CONTENTS

PART I

Be Still and Know
That He is God

THE
LOVE OF
GOD

Y ou were born to love and be loved. Did you know that?

Your purpose in life goes far beyond earning a living, taking care of your family, or just making it from day to day. You were created by God to have a fulfilling, one-on-one relationship with Him and to share this love with others. In a complex world, filled with emotional pain and complicated social problems, this purpose statement may sound simplistic, but it is not.

A lawyer and Jesus Christ once had a very important conversation: "'Teacher,' [the lawyer asked], 'which is the great commandment in the Law?'

"And He said to him, '"You shall love the Lord your God with all your heart, and with all your soul, and with all your mind.' This is the great and foremost commandment. And a second is like it, "you shall love your neighbor as yourself." On these two commandments depend the whole Law and the Prophets.'" (Matthew 22:36-40)

The people in Jesus' time, especially the teachers and legal experts, were just as concerned with "getting to the bottom line" as we are today. What is life all about? What's most important? Jesus' answer is absolutely clear: the entire point of mankind's existence comes down to love.

From the moment of your conception, and even before that, God loved you. (Ephesians 1:3-6) In your mother's womb, He put you together, nerve by nerve and cell by cell, carefully fashioning you as a unique handiwork. Psalm 139:15-16 describes God's attention to your personal formation: "My frame was not hidden from Thee, when I was made in secret, and skillfully wrought in the depths of the earth. Thine eyes have seen my unformed substance; and in Thy book they were all written, the days that were ordained for me, when as yet there was not one of them." God knows you intimately, even better than you know yourself, and He wants you to know and love Him in return.

In her book *Intimacy With God*, Cynthia Heald writes about God's desire for you: "The God who created us has not abandoned us to grope blindly through life. He has provided, at great expense, all that we need for life and godliness. God is our *personal* Creator, and He wants to be our Shepherd who protects and provides for us. He has proclaimed His love for us, and He waits only for our response."

God's goal for your life is that you come to

know Him as the one, true God. Through knowing God, you come to worship and serve Him, praising and honoring the Lover of your soul with your words and with your life. God did not have to make you; He does not "need" you in the way that you need food or water or companionship. God is complete and lacks nothing, but He chose to create You. He chose to bring you into being as a person to receive His divine affection and to give affection back to Him. To God, this fellowship means everything.

The Many Faces of Love

When you think of love, dozens of scenes may flash across your mind — a mother holding her baby tenderly, a couple walking along the beach, children playing, old friends getting together, a nurse caring for a patient. Our word for "love" includes many different relationships and varies in intensity depending on the use.

That is why it is crucial to define exactly what we mean by love before talking about the love God has for you. In Greek, the language in which the New Testament was written, there are many words for love. *Phileo* means brotherly love, the affection between family or friends. *Eros* refers to romantic or sexual love. The word used for God's love, however, is *agape*, a term absolutely distinct from the words used to describe human relationships.

Agape love is the perfect, consuming, unfathomable, unconditional love of God. It is completely unselfish, forgiving, and dedicated to your complete welfare. On your own, you cannot generate or experience agape love; it can only come from God. If you try to think of the most generous or benevolent act a human being could perform, even that does not compare with the magnitude of God's eternal, unshakable love for you.

Five times in the Old Testament, God is called a jealous God. When the Israelites were falling into idol worship, Moses reminded them about the second of the Ten Commandments. "So watch yourselves, lest you forget the covenant of the Lord your God, which He made with you, and make for yourselves a graven image [idol] in the form of anything against which the Lord your God has commanded you. For the Lord your God is a consuming fire, a jealous God." (Deuteronomy 4:23-24)

This does not mean that God is petty or selfish, wanting to keep you all for Himself in the way that people are jealous. God's "jealousy" means that God does not want you to give the chief attention and adoration of your heart to anyone else, because He loves you so much and He designed you to find total fulfillment only in a relationship with Him. No

one and no thing can satisfy the inner longing
God placed within you. Placing priority on
anything above the Lord robs both Him and
you.

God's *agape* love never ends; it is not fickle
or waning or changeable or whimsical.
Jeremiah 31:3 says: "I have loved you with an
everlasting love; therefore I have drawn you
with loving-kindness." Our affections can
change from day to day, based on mood
swings or the condition of our health or many
factors. Yet Jesus Christ is the same yesterday,
today, and forever. (Hebrews 13:8) His love is
therefore unalterable.

God Spells Love S-A-C-R-I-F-I-C-E

You've probably heard about people who
risked their lives to save others, maybe in a fire
or a crash. At a crucial moment, they disre-
garded their own safety and future to give
someone else a chance at life. Stories like these
can make you say, "Now that's love."

Jesus said something similar in John 15:13:
"Greater love has no one than this, that one
lay down his life for his friends." This is the
kind of love Jesus demonstrated when He
came to earth to die for your sins. He gave up
everything for a time on your behalf, forgoing
the honor and glory that are His due to
become a human being — God in the flesh,
fully God and fully man, (John 1.1)

9

Philippians 2:6-8 describes His incomprehensible personal sacrifice. "Although He existed in the form of God, [He] did not regard equality with God a thing to be grasped, but emptied Himself, taking the form of a bond-servant, and being made in the likeness of men. And being found in appearance as a man, He humbled Himself by becoming obedient to the point of death, even death on a cross."

Why did He go through all of this for you? He did it to get rid of the one thing that separates you from the love of God — sin. Anything in your life that is displeasing to God and contrary to His law, God calls sin, and all of us are born with sin already in our hearts. (Romans 3:23)

Sin is the big love-blocker, and only someone without sin can remove it from you. That Someone is Jesus Christ, the sinless Son of God. He literally took your place by taking your punishment. When you believe that He did this for you, placing your faith in Him as your Savior, He wipes away every ounce of guilt and wrongdoing. (John 3:16; 13:1; Romans 8:1; 1 John 4:9-10) You are covered by His love and continue to live in His love forever.

Understanding the absolute, unconditional security of His love is vital to having a free and stable relationship with Him. If you are worried that you might lose it or are unsure if you have it, you cannot rest and abide in Christ the way He wants you to, allowing Him to have control over your life. Anxiety about His love for you is a primary cause of spiritual distress for many believers, and it is a needless one.

In her book *Grace Under Pressure,* Penelope Stokes gives this reminder: "None of us 'deserves' God's grace. At our worst, we are reprobate sinners, rebelling against the Lord's purposes in our lives. At our best, we stumble and fall, and our lives seem to be a continual cycle of sin and repentance, confession and absolution. . . . When we are most aware of our shortcomings, we are also painfully aware of our undeserving.

"Yet it is our very undeserving that places us in a position to receive grace. For grace is dependent not on our character, but on the character of God. 'The Lord longs to be gracious to you,' Isaiah 30:18 says; yet we hang our heads and cannot bring ourselves to look up into His loving face."

Jesus' sacrifice is part of God's *agape* love; you cannot fall out of God's favor or lose His love as a result of anything you say or do or think. Ephesians 2:8-9 gives you this assurance: "For by grace you have been saved through faith; and that not of yourselves, it is the gift of God; not as a result of works, that no one should boast." You did not have to perform certain actions to earn His love. God loves you because He wants to, and He never changes His mind — no matter what. (Romans 5:8)

Telling God "I Love You Too"

As you feel His love surrounding you, enveloping your whole being with divine affection and unending attention, your natural response is to show Him love in return. Gratitude, adoration, closeness, respect, affection, a holy awe, tenderness — all these feelings and more can well up inside you, causing you to want to celebrate your fellowship with Him.

Worship is one way of giving praise to the Lord. Publicly and privately, you can sing, pray, study His Word, or be encouraged by other believers in the experience of coming together. Yet as vital as worship is to your relationship with God, He calls you to an expression of love that transcends this category. God calls His children to a lifestyle of obedience.

Jesus established the connection between love and obedience in John 14:23-24, when He was telling them about how life would be after He left them to return to heaven. "If anyone loves Me, he will keep My word; and My Father will love him, and We will come to him, and make Our abode with him. He who does not love Me does not keep My words; and the word which you hear is not Mine, but the Father's who sent Me."

What you do with God's Word, how much you pay attention to His directions and commands, reveals a great deal about your love for God. Jesus is not saying that if you don't obey Him you will cease to belong to Him. Once He is your Savior, you are His forever, regardless of your behavior. Obedience is not an evaluative measure of performance but an indicator of priority.

Picture a scene between a father and his young daughter. The father tells her to clean up her room, but the girl thinks she has better things to do just then and decides to ignore his instructions. In doing so, she shows a lack of respect and even a little bit of selfishness in choosing to regard her own feelings of the moment above her father's wishes. The girl still belongs to her dad, and the dad still loves her deeply, but there is a definite problem in the relationship. In order for there to be real harmony and a genuine exchange of affection, the daughter needs to learn the best way to make him happy, and that's by doing what he says.

As Jesus moves you to maturity and instills His principles into your life, you have the growing desire to do what pleases Him. Did you ever think of God as having feelings? God

does not have "faulty feelings," with weaknesses and flaws as ours do, but He is the creator of emotions. When you ignore what He
says, God allows Himself to be affected personally by your decision. Ephesians 4:30 says:
"And do not grieve the Holy Spirit of God,
by whom you were sealed for the day of
redemption."

Understand that God's commands are
good. His direction is always in your best
interest. (Matthew 7:7-11) Many of His commands, especially the ones in the Ten
Commandments, are for your own safety.
(Exodus 20) A psalmist in the Old Testament
understood the link between true joy and
obedience to God's commands. His song of
praise in Psalm 119 is filled with awe over
God's wisdom in setting up moral guidelines
that protect us from potentially devastating
effects of sin.

He writes: "Blessed are they whose ways
are blameless, who walk according to the law
of the Lord. Blessed are they who keep His
statutes and seek Him with all their heart. . . .

"I will praise You with an upright heart as I
learn Your righteous laws. . . .

"Keep me from deceitful ways; be gracious
to me through Your law. I have chosen the
way of truth; I have set my heart on Your
laws.

"I hold fast to Your statutes, O Lord; do not let me be put to shame. I run in the path of Your commands, for You have set my heart free." (Psalm 119:1-2, 7, 29-32, NIV)

Obedience is not a mechanical, dull exercise of drudgery; it is the key to a true, godly liberty that knows no boundaries.

Be a Love-Spreader

The world is starved for love. It doesn't take a survey or a study to figure out that a root cause of many social ills is a lack of genuine love. For those who do not know the love of God, the empty space in their hearts gnaws at them continually, regardless of whether they consciously acknowledge this void. Many seek to fill the space with a host of distractions or addictions, while others simply grab attention or whatever affection they can find for the moment.

When it comes to sharing God's love with others, there is no shortage of takers, and that is why you must take your role as a representative of His love so seriously. Second Corinthians 1:3-4 says: "Blessed be the God and Father of our Lord Jesus Christ, the Father of mercies and God of all comfort; who comforts us in all our affliction so that we may be able to comfort those who are in any affliction with the comfort with which we ourselves are comforted by God."

With a Savior and Friend who attends to every need and covers your life with His promise of eternal care, you have His unlimited resources at your disposal. In difficult circumstances, under stress, in times of confusion, you have a relationship with the One with the answers and the strength to see you through. Now, you have the opportunity to share this love with others. You are the ambassador who can make a difference; you are the salt of the earth and the light of the world. (2 Corinthians 5:20; Matthew 5:13-16)

Of course, it's easy to think in vague or general terms about "helping others" and "giving love." But what do these phrases mean? To whom *exactly* are you to show love? In Luke 10:30-36, in response to someone's attempt to stump Him with a tough question, Jesus told a parable about this very important issue.

"A certain man was going down from Jerusalem to Jericho; and he fell among robbers, and they stripped him and beat him, and went off leaving him half dead.

"And by chance a certain priest was going down on that road, and when he saw him, he passed by on the other side.

"And likewise a Levite also . . . passed by on the other side.

"But a certain Samaritan, who was on a

journey, came upon him; and when he saw him, he felt compassion, and came to him, and bandaged up his wounds, pouring oil and wine on them; and he put him on his own beast, and brought him to an inn, and took care of him.

". . .Which of these three do you think proved to be a neighbor to the man who fell into the robbers' hands?"

You know the answer — the good Samaritan, the interracial man who was despised by the Jews. The Samaritan had been treated badly by the people of the wounded man, yet he reached across even societal barriers to meet the need that crossed his path.

That is what Jesus wants you to do, to meet the needs He places in your way regardless of apparent obstacles. You never have to look far, but sometimes you must keep your eyes open for those in need. Hurting people do not always bear obvious wounds. If someone has emotional scars on the inside, he or she may be able to conceal them well, or possibly, this person may have adopted certain mannerisms to cover them up. Behavior that is offensive to you or that makes if difficult to be around someone may be a disguised cry for help.

Yet even if you suffer deliberate ill-treatment from someone, as the Samaritan did (indirectly), you still have the God-given obligation for ministry. Jesus explained: "'You have heard that it was said, 'You shall love your neighbor, and hate your enemy.' But I say to you, love your enemies, and pray for those who persecute you in order that you may be sons of your Father who is in heaven....

"For if you love those who love you, what reward have you? Do not even the tax-gatherers do the same? And if you greet your brothers only, what do you do more than others? Do not even the Gentiles do the same?" (Matthew 5:43-47)

It's much easier to be nice to those who are kind to you. If you have ever done something thoughtful for people who gave you only cold looks, a smart-alecky quip, or ingratitude in return, you know how demotivating such responses can be. The last thing you want to do is think about how you can be of help to them again, yet that is the mind-set Jesus calls you to have. The interests of others are to be foremost in your mind, in spite of their attitudes toward you. (Philippians 2:3-5)

Look in the Mirror

Before you can really be an effective love-giver, however, you must learn to love yourself properly. How you treat others depends in large part on how you love yourself. No, this isn't "feel good" phraseology from a pop psychology book. Refer again to Matthew 22:39:

"And a second [command] is like it, 'You shall love your neighbor *as yourself*'" (emphasis mine).

Jesus is talking about treating others with the same respect and concern you naturally give yourself. If you have a low self-esteem, devaluing your worth in God's eyes or paralyzed by a sense of inadequacy, then you are not equipped to reach out to someone else. You are a needy person yourself, and your interactions with others often become attempts to fill your own wants rather than satisfying theirs. You run the very real risk of becoming a "user," perhaps even without knowing it.

The best treatment for a low self-esteem, a subject which cannot be dealt with in detail here, is to supply your thinking with truths about your "Jesus-esteem." Find verses in the Bible that reaffirm your value in His eyes and memorize them. (Psalm 139, Matthew 10:29-31, and 1 Samuel 16:7b provide a good start.) Feelings of shame, inferiority, or uselessness, cannot stand up to the words of Scripture, and over time your thought patterns are transformed and made new.

Loving others is no simple task, and no one knows that better than Jesus. He even tells you to expect some hassles and grief along the way (John 15:20-21) He took more undeserved abuse than anyone else will ever suffer, and He is with you at all times to infuse your spirit with His strength and tenacity. (Matthew 28:20) You cannot love out of your own resources and trying to do so means walking down a sure path to spiritual depletion and emotional burnout.

Let the Lord pour His love through you. Being the vessel in His capable hands relieves you of countless stressful burdens He never intended for you to carry.

Profile of a Prodigal

Jesus's Parable of the Prodigal Son coming home to his waiting father furnishes an excellent picture of how God's love can operate in and through your life. The younger son had scorned his father's provision, asked for his inheritance early, and headed out of town to live life his way. After the son's money ran out, however, so did his so-called friends, and before long he was destitute and alone.

This once-rich Jewish boy now slopped hogs for a living, near starvation and wondering if his father would take him back as a servant. Read what happened when he decided to return home: "And he got up and came to his father. But while he was still a long way off, his father saw him, and felt compassion for him, and ran and embraced him, and kissed him.

"And the son said to him, 'Father, I have

sinned against heaven and in your sight; I am no longer worthy to be called your son.'

"But the father said to his slaves, 'Quickly bring out the best robe and put it on him, and put a ring on his hand and sandals on his feet; and bring the fattened calf, kill it, and let us eat and be merry; for this son of mine was dead, and has come to life again; he was lost, and has been found.'" (Luke 15:20-24)

This touching scene reveals three key qualities of enduring love, patterned after God's unconditional acceptance.

(1) *Love is not a feeling or passing emotion — it's a commitment.* If the father had let the feelings of the moment get the best of him, he might have reacted out of hurt or anger. The ups and downs of waiting surely took a toll on his emotions, but his love was not based on his mood that day. His commitment as a father determined his actions and shaped his passionate response.

(2) *Love is an affirmation of belonging, competence, and worth.* The son must have been shocked when he felt his father's strong embrace around his dirty body. Working in a pig sty doesn't make one very appealing, but his appearance didn't stop his excited dad. The father wanted the son to know that he was special, priceless, irreplaceable. Real love says, "you're always accepted here."

(3) *Love continues to care, even when it is rejected or ignored.* This father loved his son just as much when he walked out the door as when he walked in the door. The father did not consider all those years of love while raising him to be a waste; even if the son had never returned, his love would not have diminished.

Again, can you see how a love that lasts is really a picture of God's *agape* love? In fact, in this parable, the father represents God the Father, whom you can call your personal Father. (Romans 8:15; Galatians 4:6) And you're right — nobody can love this way on his own. Eventually, your human patience and long-suffering will run out, especially in the face of maltreatment. That is why you need to rely on the Holy Spirit to administer God's love through you. He enables you to go beyond what you want or desire to treat others solely for their good.

The Power of Love

No other power on earth has the sheer potency of genuine love.

It can melt the hardest heart and the hardest head in a way that logic or language or law can never match. Love can persuade when all other means fail, and without love, any endeavor is meaningless.

In 1 Corinthians 13:1-2, Paul writes: "If I

speak with the tongues of men and of angels, but do not have love, I have become a noisy gong or a clanging cymbal. And if I have the gift of prophecy, and know all mysteries and all knowledge; and if I have all faith, so as to remove mountains, but do not have love, I am nothing."

After this description, you might suppose that Paul thought of love only in broad and lofty terms, but in the next several verses he paints a picture of down-to-earth ways of pointing others to the greatest Lover of all — the Lord Jesus Christ. Notice that Paul does not try to define the awesome force of love in technical terms; he simply tells us how it looks and how it acts.

The following list is a sampling of the qualities in verses four through eight of the the love chapter, 1 Corinthians 13.

◆ *Love is patient.* This means waiting in line when you'd rather find a way to cut in; not venting your frustration on a harried cashier after you've waited in line; taking time to help someone who needs one-on-one attention. Patience says, "I'll move at your pace and fit in with your schedule."

◆ *Love does not act unbecomingly.* The rules of common courtesy fit into this category nicely. You do not hear as much about etiquette these days, but being polite is a sure way to communicate respect, a fundamental part of love. Holding open a door, carrying a package, passing food at the table, not interrupting in conversations, having good poise and grooming, excercising discretion in public — the list goes on. Courtesty says, "I care about your comfort and don't want to offend you."

◆ *Love does not brag and is not arrogant.* Have you ever caught yourself "tooting your own horn"? It's easy to do when you allow your focus to stay too long on self or when you're looking for a pat on the back. The Lord wants to help you cultivate the attitude of Philippians 2:3: "But with humility of mind let each of you regard one another as more important than himself." You need never be a doormat, but you should seek to build up and affirm those around you, even at the expense of receiving praise for yourself.

What is the meaning of life? It's exactly what Jesus said it is — receiving the love of God and allowing Him to use you to give it to someone else. Let Galatians 5:6b become a personal theme verse:

"The only thing that counts is faith expressing itself through love."

DISCOVERING GOD'S WILL

"Should I marry this girl? I really think God has brought us together, but I would like to know God's mind on our future."

"I was offered a new job in another state. There are a lot of pluses about it. Can God help me make a wise decision?"

"My daughter is a high school senior and has the opportunity to attend several colleges. How can I know which one is right for her?"

While the Scriptures do not give a precise formula for discovering God's will in these intensely personal circumstances, they do plainly tell us that we have a Guide, Jesus Christ, who will lead us in the right direction and help us make fundamentally sound choices in major and minor decisions.

We are enjoined by God to rationally seek His will for our lives (our part), but ultimately we must depend upon Him for sure and certain guidance (His part). We do not have all the details, but we do have an all-knowing, all-loving, and all-powerful Guide, Jesus Christ, who promises guidance to His followers (His part).

Keep this verity in mind as we examine the principles and precepts of knowing and doing the will of God. You want guidance, and God will provide it. Supremely though, you desire to better know the personal Guide who unerringly leads you in righteous paths. This is the right and true context for seeking the will of God.

Does God Have a Plan for Me?

Before the world was formed, God had a precise plan for the salvation of its inhabitants. (Ephesians 1:3-4) He executed it through the ages, choosing the Hebrew people as the ones to whom He would give His laws and through whom He would send His Son, Jesus Christ, to suffer, die, and be raised from the dead for the sins of the world. The church, comprised of believers in Christ, is the visible post-resurrection witness to an unbelieving world.

God has a plan for the material universe also. This earth and heaven will one day give way to an entirely new creation. (2 Peter 3:10-12)

The Bible is likewise clear that God has a will for individuals. He chose Joseph at a young age to rule over Egypt, despite the tumultuous, no doubt confusing years of prison and isolation. He handpicked Moses to lead the Hebrews out of Egypt. He selected a young shepherd boy to be the unlikely but prominent king of Israel. The apostle Paul was sent to preach to the Gentiles, Peter to the Jews.

"So then do not be foolish," Paul exhorted the church at Ephesus and us today, "but understand what the will of the Lord is." (Ephesians 5:17)

He prayed for the believers at Colossae to be "filled with the knowledge of His will in all spiritual wisdom and understanding." (Colossians 1:9)

Jesus told us to pray with the idea firmly in mind for the Father's will to be done in the here and now as it is in heaven. (Matthew 6:10)

James encourages us to ask God for wisdom (inferring His will) when we lack understanding, with the assurance that God will respond with a personal reply. (James 1:5)

Since we can know and do the will of God it stands to reason that He has a thoughtful, ordered design for our lives. Indeed, once we are saved, we are rocketed into an incredible adventure of discovering a life of significant meaning and purpose. There are unpleasant seasons of trouble and perplexity, but they too are part of our new spiritual journey of trusting Christ. We gain a new identity as God's "workmanship, created in Christ Jesus for good works, which God prepared beforehand, that we should walk in them." (Ephesians 2:10)

Paul E. Little writes in *Affirming the Will of God:* "It is important to understand at the outset that God has plan and purpose for your life. This is one of the sensational aspects of being a Christian—to know that your life can be tied into God's plan and purpose not only for time but for eternity."

The Big Picture

"Swell," you may think, "if God has a plan for me, then I definitely have a problem breaking His code." I can identify with that sentiment since I, too, have sought some very specific guidance from the Lord and was met with seeming silence.

I have learned a valuable lesson in these times, however. I can become so entangled with all the details that I lose sight of the big picture. And what is that?

"And we know that God causes all things to work together for good to those who love God, to those who are called according to His purpose. For whom He foreknew, He also predestined to become conformed to the image of His Son. . . . " (Romans 8:28-29)

The big picture is that I should glorify Christ. God accomplishes this by using all that happens, pro and con, to mold me into Christ's likeness. The more I view my circumstances in this light, the more crystallized my thought process becomes as I seek God's will.

"Lord, I need Your guidance in this area of

LIVING
CLOSE TO
GOD

*Finding His Power in
Your Everyday Life*

CHARLES STANLEY

INSPIRATIONAL PRESS

NEW YORK

Previously published in twelve separate volumes:

The Love of God, Discovering God's Will, Spirit Filled Living, The Power of Prayer, The Heart of Praise, Freedom Through Forgiveness, How to Triumph Over Temptation, Overcoming Adversity, and *How to Handle Fear:* copyright © 1995 by Charles F. Stanley.

Growing in Faith, Spiritual Warfare, and *Beyond Bitterness:* copyright © 1996 by Charles F. Stanley.

Acknowledgments for *Overcoming Adversity*:

Unless otherwise indicated Scriptures are from the *New American Standard Bible,* © the Lockman Foundation 1960, 1962, 1963, 1968, 1971, 1972, 1973, 1975, 1977. Other references are from J.B. Phillips: *The New Testament in Modern English,* Revised Edition (PH), © J. B. Phillips, 1958, 1960, 1972, permission of Macmillan Publishing Co. and Collins Publishers.

Acknowledgments for all other volumes:

Unless otherwise indicated Scriptures are from the *New American Standard Bible,* © the Lockman Foundation 1960, 1962, 1963, 1968, 1971, 1972, 1973, 1975, 1977. Other references are from the *Holy Bible, New International Version* ® (NIV). Copyright © 1973, 1978, 1984 by International Bible Society. Used by permission of Zondervan Publishing House. All rights reserved.

First Inspirational Press edition published in 1999.

Inspirational Press
A division of BBS Publishing Corporation
386 Park Avenue South
New York, NY 10016.

Inspirational Press is a registered trademark of BBS Publishing Corporation.

Published by arrangement with Chariot Victor Publishing, a division of Cook Communications Ministries.

Library of Congress Catalog Card Number: 98-75431

ISBN: 0-88486-239-9

Printed in the United States of America.

my finances. However You lead, my priority is to use my funds to honor You. I understand You are the owner and I am the steward."

There's a tremendous spiritual freedom in this approach. If I am more concerned with God's glory than I am with my need, then chances are I really do want His will more than my own.

It's amazing how this mind-set filters out selfish motives and misguided thinking in seeking the will of the Lord. It focuses our attention on pleasing Christ as opposed to ourselves. The answers, whenever and however they come, are cause for praise and worship as well as meeting practical needs.

In her book, *A Slow and Certain Light,* Elisabeth Elliot terms this the "recognition of who God is" factor. "The first condition is the recognition of God Himself. It is not who does He think I am, but who do I think He is. I confess that after many years I am still having to go back often to this, to Lesson 1 in the school of faith. I forget what I learned, I start out on false premises: who I am, what I need, why my case is special, what I'm hoping for, what I pray for, or something—anything but the thing that matters most: who God is."

What Determines What I Hear?

How we perceive God's character colors the process of knowing God's plan. Two persons can seek God's direction for identical requests yet reach dissimilar conclusions. The difference lies in their perspective on the nature of God.

Do You Think of God As:

A loving or demanding Father? If you feel you can never measure up to God's exacting standards and are hounded with an unshakable sense of guilt and condemnation, then your perception of God is skewed. God's wrath was heaved upon His own Son at the cross, so you might walk under the canopy of His unceasing and unfailing love. Even the discipline of God in dealing with believers is motivated by love and concern for the well-being of His children. You are accepted by Him regardless of your performance. His love for you can never be exhausted.

An intimate or distant Friend? A distant friend is only casually interested in you and really doesn't want to hear the particulars. God wants to build an intimate relationship with you for eternity. When I spoke on this topic during a missionary trip, a young student from Russia approached me after I finished and said he had known Christ as His Savior and Lord, but had never truly related to Jesus as his Friend. His relationship with God changed dramatically as a result. God *is* your very best Friend.

A patient or intolerant Teacher? When you blow it, do you hear God say, "Why do you keep messing up? Can't you get it through your thick skull what you are supposed to do?" God is not an intolerant Teacher. His input is more like this when we need correction: "Let Me show you why you failed and where you went wrong so that you won't become discouraged and repeat the same behavior. I want you to grow spiritually. I will help you no matter how often you stumble."

A generous or reluctant Provider? God is not stingy. He is not calculating how little you can get or the minimum He will do for you. God does not operate that way. He provides according to "His riches in glory in Christ Jesus" (Philippians 4:19), His way of expressing an inexhaustible supply of strength, joy, peace, patience, loving-kindness and goodness. You do not have to wrench a response from a celestial tightwad. You come to One who does more than you can even imagine or think. (Ephesians 3:20)

Discerning God's Will

God understands our need to make intelligent decisions about very practical concerns. He wants us to keep the big picture in mind and concentrate on our relationship with Him, but He is a God of the details as well.

He told Abraham where to move. He'll help

you know if you should be in Topeka or Nashville. He gave Moses a new job description. He'll guide you as you make a midlife career change.

I seriously doubt God will use visions, dreams, or some sort of supernatural phenomenon to communicate His plan. That was His method long ago, but we have a better way today of knowing what the mind of Christ is for the decisions we must make.

The Scriptures

The Bible is the cornerstone for knowing God's guidance. Any quest for guidance apart from the light of God's Word is perilous.

The Scripture is God's revelation to men. It is the progressive unfolding of His wisdom and ways. For instance, how would we know the plan of salvation apart from the Bible?

The psalmist wrote: "Thy word is a lamp to my feet, and a light to my path." (Psalm 119:105) He realized that as he meditated on the Scriptures he would "have more insight than all [his] teachers." (Psalm 119:99)

The Scriptures tell what God's moral will is. They tell us what to do and what not to. It is God's will that we maintain a grateful heart (1 Thessalonians 5:18) and live in a holy manner. (1 Thessalonians 4:3) Conversely, it is not

God's will that we grumble and complain or engage in immoral thoughts or actions.

These things are plain, but often we over-look the very basics of Scripture in seeking to know God's will. It's pointless to ask God if we should be involved in church on Sunday or spend fifty-two weekends a year at the lake. (Hebrews 10:24)

The principles of God are also rooted in the Bible. They provide spiritual parameters which at some point we will intersect in our decision-making.

We may be in a serious quandary over whether or not to purchase an automobile. The Bible doesn't have any information on Chevrolets or Fords, but it has a lot say that is pertinent. God's principles on debt, savings, and contentment all factor into the answer.

The Scriptures are also where God's promises are revealed. Some are conditional, dependent on our obedience; others simply tell us what God will do if we trust Him.

Philippians 4:19 assures me that God will meet my needs. I don't always know how or when, but I can count on the resources of God for the demands of modern living. That is an incredible promise that settles and sustains me.

One of the best suggestions I can make is to

spend time daily meditating on God's Word. Your mind will be renewed in this exercise and the principles and promises will become part of your new way of thinking. When you need to know God's will in a matter, you have a tremendous advantage for you can recall much of what God has said in His Word. This also prevents what someone has called the "lucky dip method" of opening the Scripture and looking for a verse to guide you. That's terribly unorthodox and incompatible with spiritual maturity. It may work sometimes, but don't count on it.

The Holy Spirit and Prayer

The Holy Spirit has been placed by God within each believer as a divine teacher, to instruct us and guide us. (John 14:26; John 16:13)

Paul told the church at Rome that the Holy Spirit was interceding on its behalf to help it do the right thing when the answer wasn't obvious. (Romans 8:26) He unveils the mind of Christ to us. (1 Corinthians 2:12, 16)

It is comforting to know that I am not left to my own clever devices to know the will of God. I am not left in the dark, destined to grope for answers until perhaps I accidentally hit the light switch.

As a member of the Trinity, the Holy Spirit has the designated responsibility to open my mind and heart to understand the will of God.

We must never underestimate His role. I encourage you to affirm your reliance on the Holy Spirit as you seek the will of the Father. Don't expect goose bumps; just realize He will provide you with the truth you need.

The realm of prayer is where the Holy Spirit operates most productively. After all, we are asking God to know His will and prayer is asking.

It was the ministry of the Holy Spirit working in tandem with prayer that set the stage for Paul and Barnabas' first missionary journey. (Acts 13:1-3)

I cannot think of a major decision in my life that has not been made without a season of deliberate, focused prayer. Petitions presented in a spirit of humility and trust are instantly acknowledged by God and in time answered.

Make sure your prayers are specific. Get to the point. "Lord, I need You to show me if You want Bill to be my business partner." The plainer you are, the easier the answer will be to recognize.

"God insists that we ask," wrote Catherine Marshall in *The Adventure of Prayer*, "not because He needs to know our situation, but because we need the spiritual discipline of asking. . . . The reason many of us retreat into

vague generalities when we pray is not
because we think too highly of God, but
because we think too little."

Counsel and Circumstances

Proverbs is the book of wisdom which
means the practical application of knowledge.
A collection of verses affirms the value of
godly advice.

" A man's counsel is sweet to his friend."
(Proverbs 27:9)

"In abundance of counselors there is victory." (Proverbs 24:6)

"Prepare plans by consultation."
(Proverbs 20:18)

Insights from a mature Christian friend
often can help you sift through the pros and
cons of decision-making. Individuals with
whom you have developed a mutual accountability relationship can be especially helpful.

I remember one specific incident when God
used the wisdom of others as a catalyst for His
healing. I had sensed for several months that
God was dealing with my life and ministry. I
prayed frequently, asking God to enlighten
me, and studied His Word. Still, I had no real
sense of His direction.

I called four of my closest friends one afternoon and asked them to meet me the next

morning. They cleared their schedule and we gathered to pray and talk.

After many hours, one of the men whom I knew well asked me this question: "Charles, how would you feel if your father picked you up in his arms and said, 'I love you'?" I instantly burst into tears. My father died when I was a baby and my stepfather was an angry, hostile man who never expressed love. At that moment, God showed me how much He really did care for me and that I needed to receive and experience His love each day. And I can honestly say my life and preaching have never been the same since that encounter.

I'm sure God could have revealed all of this in another manner, but He chose to use wise, godly friends as His means of opening my eyes to His truth. Likewise, God has put certain people in your life who can be of great value in helping you know His will.

I might add that the arrangement of circumstances can be indicators of God's guidance. Obviously, the Lord works through events and providentially orchestrates them for your good. If you are praying about buying a good used car with low mileage and you discover in a conversation with your neighbor that he would like to sell his car, which happens to match your desires, it's a good idea to check it out.

You may find it's the ideal automobile that fits your taste and your budget. But you may discover in reviewing maintenance and repair records that it is not mechanically reliable. Neither circumstance nor counsel alone should ever determine God's guidance. They must work in conjunction with persevering prayer, dependence on the Holy Spirit, and immersion in God's Word.

George Sweeting writes in *How to Discover the Will of God*:

"Often guidance in the will of God will come to us in the normal circumstances of life, through open and closed doors. But be careful not to give this area more consideration than it deserves. Satan can also open and shut doors of opportunity. Gather all the facts, and prayerfully seek the mind of God."

When the Fog Remains

Since seeking God's will is not a science that operates within predictable parameters, it can be difficult to discern whether or not we are progressing in the right direction.

God asks us to wait for His answer, and well we should. But He can also use the fog of uncertainty in a corrective manner to rechart our course, rethink our request, or examine our relationship with Him.

I have found several common factors that

can obscure the unfolding of His plan.

◆ *Disobedience*

The eighty-first Psalm is a sad commentary on "what might have been" for the nation of Israel. God desired to supply their many needs in a bountiful way (vs. 16) but the people cut off His supply through their rebellious, disobedient spirit. (vs. 11-13) If there is an area of willful, stubborn disobedience in your life that you refuse to address, then knowing God's will probably will remain perplexing. Remember, His plan always revolves around the quality of your relationship with Him.

◆ *Doubt*

The Christian life is a journey of faith. It's impossible to please God apart from confident trust in His ability. (Hebrews 11:6) If you ask for guidance, don't doubt for a moment that God will give it. He bestows it "without reproach" (James 1:5), without condemnation for past failures or mistakes. If you are unsure that God will direct you, then why ask Him? (We all have passing moments of doubt. James speaks here of persistent unbelief in God's ability.)

◆ *Manipulation*

God cannot and will not be manipulated. In 1 Samuel 13, Saul failed to wait on Samuel as the prophet had instructed and instead took matters into his own hands by offering a sacrifice. His manipulative actions forfeited his kingship over Israel, and God selected David as his successor. When seeking Christ's direction, refuse the temptation to "help God" resolve the issue. Take only those measures that are within proper ethical and biblical guidelines. You never lose by waiting on God to supply your need.

◆ *Wrong Motivation*

James tells us that if we ask God for an answer without the right motivation, then our petitions will fall flat. (James 4:3) You may seek God for the right private school for your child to attend. If your purpose is for your child's spiritual and educational well-being and it fits within your budget, then your motivation is probably pure. But if keeping up with the Joneses who also send their child to private school has seeped into your thinking, then you need to reexamine your motivation. Ask the right thing for the right reason. Filter everything through a quality, daily relationship with Christ.

◆ *Ignoring Responsibilities*

In guidance there is always our part and God's part. Occasionally, we confuse the two (this is where manipulation comes in), but in most cases common sense is the rule.

If we need a job and sit at home while we

wait for the president of some corporation to find our unlisted number and call, we have failed to fulfill our responsibility for diligence and initiative. (Proverbs 19:15)

◆ *Rejecting the Channel or Means*

You have a financial need. You've prayed about it and asked God to supply the funds. A former business associate calls you at home and informs you he is sending you a check for just the amount you need. Instead of celebrating, however, you decline the offer because it is the same individual who once maliciously damaged your reputation at the office. Pride prevents you from accepting the channel of God's supply. Remember the story of Naaman the leper? King of Aram, Naaman came to Israel to visit the prophet Elisha. He had heard of Elisha's miracles through one of his slaves and came to him for a cure. When Elisha prescribed that Naaman dip himself seven times in the Jordan River for a remedy, the king was outraged. Only on the wise advice of one of his servants did he obey Elisha and see his leprosy instantly removed. Pride had brought Naaman perilously close to rejecting God's plan. Keep an open mind as to how God will answer your requests since His resources are infinite.

◆ *Redirecting Our Life*

At times, the way seems to be dark even

when we have done all we can with the right motive, waiting patiently for God's response. If this is the case, consider that the Lord may be redirecting your life. The job you really wanted just never seems to materialize because God is orchestrating a career change for you that will place you around people who nurture your faith. The apostle Paul had tried to take his missionary team into parts of Asia Minor, but the Holy Spirit prevented him. (Acts 16:6-7) Why? God had plans for Paul in Greece and ultimately Rome. And it appears that Peter was used by the Lord to minister the gospel in Asia. (1 Peter 1:1)

Remember These Things

Don't assume because you run into trouble that you have done the wrong thing. Paul wound up in prison or was beaten and harassed in most of the cities where he preached. Adversity did not mean he had made a wrong decision, only that God was molding his character through suffering and trials.

Don't become neurotic about missing the will of God. God's plan is not a tightrope upon which one misstep will hurl you into oblivion. He cares too much for you to put you into a perpetual state of fretting and anxiety. He'll let you know what His plans are as you relax and know that He is God (Psalm 46:10); He is well able to communicate His will to you. When we miss the mark, there is the safety net of forgiveness and restoration. Mark abandoned Paul on his first missionary journey, yet he was one of the men Paul summoned as he waited for execution in a Roman prison. (2 Timothy 4:11)

Don't major on minors. God really isn't interested in the color of your automobile, the type of soft drink you consume, whether you drive the scenic or interstate route to work, the brand of running shoes you wear, or other such minor matters. He leaves such things to personal preferences, equipping you with a sound, capable intellect to make reasonable decisions.

Don't expect God to reveal His life plan for you all at once. Knowing God's will is a step-by-step, day-by-day process in which we develop Christian character and maturity. The Christian life is one of faith, and that involves constant dependence on God.

Don't depend on feelings. Certainly God wants us to enjoy His serenity as we seek His guidance. But "feeling" God's peace is not the determining factor in knowing God's will. I'm not sure how wonderful Abraham felt when God called him to a new country, but he obeyed. God may grant you His peace in the decision-making process, but be principle-centered rather than peace-centered.

Do take the next logical step. Don't get caught in the "paralysis of analysis," but instead keep up the daily routine, your spiritual eyes and ears alert to God's small surprises. Waiting on God is not passive, but going about your tasks, knowing that God is orchestrating all for your good.

Do engage in thanksgiving. Praise keeps us expectant and hopeful and is a terrific antidote against discouragement. Worship rivets our attention on the capability of the Guide.

Do maintain a lifestyle of helping others. The scriptural injunction to do good to others (even putting their interests above our own) keeps our needs in perspective. And interaction with other members of Christ's body often is part of the equation of God's response to our petitions.

Do approach the process of knowing God's will as an adventure. Paul Tournier, the Swiss psychiatrist, said: "Life is an adventure directed by God." Fullness of joy is a distinct trait of the Christian, and discovering God's will should only increase that sanguinity.

Do factor in your personal desires and tastes. The person who delights himself in relationship with the Savior can find his personal desire frequently fulfilled. (Psalm 37:4) The man whose heart is bent toward God most often finds his desires are in harmony with God's. There is no dichotomy.

SPIRIT FILLED LIVING

I will ask the Father, and He will give you another Helper, that He may be with you forever; that is the Spirit of truth . . . (John 14:16-17).

Realizing There Was a Need

Several months before I graduated from seminary, I was invited to preach at a small church outside Hendersonville, North Carolina. Since the church didn't have a pastor and because my wife and I were vacationing in the area, I thought it would be nice to take advantage of the opportunity and gain some on-the-job training. The church's response to the sermons was very positive. In fact, they liked what they heard so much that they asked me to become their next pastor.

Initially, I was taken aback by their request and declined, saying that I had another year of seminary to complete. However, they assured me they were willing to wait until I graduated. Immediately, I began praying for God's guidance in making my decision, and it wasn't long before He made it clear that I should accept the call.

It so happened that a small Bible college was located across the street from the church.

I didn't think about it much, but a month before my graduation, the director called me to ask if I would consider teaching two classes during the fall semester. One class dealt with evangelism, and the other was a course in preaching.

"Preaching!" I thought. "I've only preached six or seven sermons in my entire life. How could I possibly teach a sermon preparation class?" Once more I went to God in prayer, and again I felt Him leading me to accept the position.

My wife and I arrived in Fruitland, North Carolina, in June of 1957, where I immediately began serving as pastor. However, whenever thoughts of the approaching fall semester crept into my mind, an uneasiness filled my heart. I could sense something was missing or was not right, but at this point I didn't know what it was.

As the summer drew to a close and I was forced to face the reality of teaching college-level classes, something happened inside of me. I was already struggling with thoughts of inadequacy, but there was a growing desire to draw closer to God. It was at this point that I rediscovered Dr. R.A. Torrey's book *The Person and Work of the Holy Spirit*. I had read it in seminary, but found myself consuming it with a new hunger. The previous two years had been spent praying to know all there was to know about God, and I believed He had something more to teach me. My hopes were that Dr. Torrey's book would unlock the truth.

Something More

It quickly became evident from Torrey's writing that God calls men and women to follow the leading of His Spirit. He has a plan in mind for each of our lives. However, the only way to know His plan is by knowing Him. The Holy Spirit is an agent of communication. It is through Him that God provides wisdom and knowledge for every situation we face.

Torrey writes, "[The Spirit] guides in the details of daily life, and service as to where to go and where not to go, what to do and what not to do." I had spent years studying God's Word, but my life was limited because I had not developed my relationship with the Holy Spirit. Thus His work in my life was limited.

"It is possible for us to have the unerring guidance of the Holy Spirit at every turn of life," explains Torrey. This means not just in "forms of Christian work, but in all the affairs of life — business, study, everything we have to do."

The reality of Christ's words penetrated my thinking. "I will ask the Father, and He will give you another *Helper*, that He may be with you forever; that is the *Spirit of truth*, whom the world cannot receive, because it does not behold Him or know Him, but you know Him because He abides with you, and will be in you. I will not leave you as orphans; I will come to you. . . . In that day you shall know that I am in My Father, and you in Me, and I in you. He who has my commandments and keeps them, he it is who loves Me; and he who loves Me shall be loved by My Father, and I will love him, and will disclose Myself to him" (John 14:16-21).

Surrender — The Pathway to God

"The Spirit also helps our weakness; for we do not know how to pray as we should, but the Spirit Himself intercedes for us. . . ."

Romans 8:26

Looking back, I now know God engineered the circumstances of my life so I would be forced to come to a point of desperation. The thought of teaching college courses added immeasurable stress and underscored my need for God in every area of my life.

If you had asked me if I believed in the Holy Spirit, I would have answered an affirming yes, and I also would have quoted 1 Corinthians 6:19 as proof. "Do you not know that your body is a temple of the Holy Spirit who is in you, whom you have from God, and that you are not your own?"

However, I wasn't as sure of the Spirit's *role* in my life. I was struck with a deep desire to understand and apply all that God had for me. It was Friday afternoon and my first class was scheduled to begin on Monday. I had read, studied, memorized, prayed, fasted, and pleaded with God to change my life, but the sensation of lacking an important element in my spiritual walk with Christ remained.

I began meditating on two verses in 1 John. "And this is the confidence which we have before Him, that, if we ask anything according to His will, He hears us. And if we know that He hears us in whatever we ask, we know that we have the requests which we have asked from Him" (1 John 5:14-15).

Then I prayed, "Lord, You promised that if I ask anything according to Your will, You will hear me. I know it's not Your will for me to be frustrated and struggle with inadequacy. I believe You want me to experience the power of Your Holy Spirit. I have done all I know to do, and I don't want to go into that classroom on Monday unprepared. I also know You don't want me to quit. So, I'm going to trust You because I don't know what else to do. I surrender my entire life to You. Take me and use me in whatever way You know is best. "

Immediately, confidence and assurance began growing inside of me. Something had changed. The feelings of fear and confusion

I had felt that morning vanished. I didn't see stars or a vision or speak in tongues or do anything except trust God, but I was struck by the revelation of what I had been doing for the past several months. I had been so busy *trying* to convince God to provide some physical manifestation to confirm what He was doing that I almost missed the reality of His presence in my life.

The truth I discovered was this: A person who lives a Spirit-filled life lives by faith, not by sight. There's no need to beg God for anything. He has already provided all we need to live the Spirit-filled life. But what we have to do is surrender ourselves to the Spirit's control and then trust Him to guide us into all truth. The issue is one of faith, and not one of seeking physical evidence.

*"If you then, being evil, know how
to give good gifts to your children, how much
more shall your heavenly Father give the Holy
Spirit to those who ask Him?"*

Luke 11:13

Someone to Come Alongside Us

The Spirit's role is one of guidance, support, and prayer. When we are walking in step with His leading, He illuminates our minds with the truth of God's Word. Jesus told His disciples: "I will ask the Father, and He will give you another Helper . . ." (John 14:16).

The Greek word for Helper is *parakletos*. It means "one who will come along aside you." W.E. Vine writes in *The Expanded Vine's Expository Dictionary of New Testament Words* that the entire thought behind the word "suggests the capability or adaptability for giving aid."

Jesus wanted to guide my life through the presence of the Holy Spirit. There was no need for me to feel inadequate or frightened in any venture as long as I knew two important facts: I was where I was as a result of following Him, and He was with me. Many of us make the mistake of jumping ahead of God and doing something He never intended for us to do.

I was not alone — nor did I have to depend on my human strength and wisdom to get me by. Jesus is my Source of strength, and I poured myself out to Him in prayer. I knew that if I would trust Him, He would show me how to teach and instruct those future pastors. What a marvelous inexpressible impact God has on our lives.

When I stepped into class on Monday, I was filled with excitement, yes, but there was also a new theme building in my life — a theme that would lead me to an even deeper commitment to Jesus Christ. Oswald Chambers writes, "The Holy Spirit is the one who makes everything Jesus did for you real in your life."

And when [Jesus] had said this,
He breathed on them, and said to them,
"Receive the Holy Spirit."

John 20:22

The Road Beyond

Throughout the day, I prayed, "Holy Spirit, I can't do this, but You can do it through me. Equip me for the work You have called me to do." God did just that. The more I became aware of my inadequacies and prayed for His help, the more He strengthened me to meet the challenge.

C.S. Lewis once wrote, "God gives His gifts where He finds the vessels empty enough to receive them." When I began emptying myself of me — my selfish desires and habits — the Holy Spirit was free to live out His life through me. I no longer stifled His work by wanting to do things my way.

I began to live a life of deeper faith. And as I walked through the hours of the day, God guided me through the indwelling of the Holy Spirit. Being led by Him brought a new sense of contentment to my heart. I realized that in letting go of my human wants, I received an even greater blessing, an awareness of God's Spirit living within me. This is the essence of the Christian life. It is a walk of faith; but more than that, it is living the Spirit-filled life.

Most of us have little trouble accepting this concept when it is connected with our salvation. However, when it comes to trusting God with day-to-day matters the story often changes. We take matters into our own hands and then complain when circumstances become skewed and we don't sense the presence of the Holy Spirit in what others are doing.

His Presence in You

The Holy Spirit is more than a sensation or a "feeling"; He is the third Person of the Trinity. The same Spirit of God who abided with Jesus throughout His earthly ministry is the One who now abides in the heart of each believer.

In the book *After the Spirit Comes,* pastor and author Jack Taylor writes, "It may be said then, without being irreverent, that the Holy Spirit is for us the presence of Jesus Christ, the spiritual presence of Jesus Himself. . . . We are indwelt of the Spirit of God who is the living Essence of Jesus in us."

Jesus told His disciples: "I will ask the Father, and He will give you another Helper, that He may be with you forever; that is the Spirit of truth, whom the world cannot receive, because it does not behold Him or know Him, but you know Him because He abides with you, and will be in you" (John 14:16-17).

Jesus made this promise based on His Father's ability. While many people try to argue the need for a "second experience," such as a baptism in the Holy Spirit, Scripture makes it clear that when we accept Christ as our Savior, His Spirit comes to indwell us. The question is not how much of the Holy Spirit *we* have, but how much of us does *He* have.

A Spirit-filled life is a life of surrender, of yielding oneself to God's control. The more we allow God to work in us, the more we see the evidence of His Spirit working within us.

But when He, the Spirit of truth, comes, He will guide you into all the truth. . . ."

John 16:13

Our Guide through Every Phase of Life

After years of living a life of surrender, Catherine Marshall writes in *The Helper*, "From my own experience and that of many others, I know the Spirit's guidance is just as real in our century as it was in Paul's day. . . . The Spirit cannot guide us, however, as long as we insist on finding our own way. It is as if we, groping alone in the dark, are offered a powerful lantern to light our path, but refuse it, preferring to stumble along striking one flickering match after the other. First we have to ask the Spirit to lead us; then by an act of will place our life situations and our future in

His hands; and then trust that He will get His instructions through to us."

God is concerned about every aspect of your life — all that you do, think, and seek to accomplish in life. This is why He sent His Spirit to be with you. We never have to suffer with loneliness or fear or rejection because a personal loving part of the Trinity is with us.

He never tires of us coming to Him. In James He says, "If any of you lacks wisdom, let him ask of God, who gives to all men generously and without reproach, and it will be given to him. But let him ask in faith without any doubting, for the one who doubts is like the surf of the sea driven and tossed by the wind. For let not that man expect that he will receive anything from the Lord . . ." (James 1:5-7).

Torrey reminds us, "There must be an entire renunciation of the wisdom of the flesh. *We must really desire to know God's way and be willing at any cost to do [His] will.* This is implied in the word 'ask.'" Our prayers need to be sincere and open toward God's will. "There is nothing," writes Torrey, "that goes so far to make our minds clear in the discernment of God's will as revealed by His Spirit as an absolutely surrendered will."

Once you ask God for something, whether it's guidance for the future or help in meeting a material need, you can confidently expect an answer in one of three ways — yes, no, or wait. Catherine Marshall writes, "When the Holy Spirit is working in us, the mighty providence of God is always working outside of us in perfect correspondence and preparation." Because God always has His best in mind for us, we can know without hesitation that our external circumstances play an important role in modeling and shaping our lives.

Take a moment to think about your life by answering the following two questions:

Have I yielded every area of my life to God, or is there a corner of resistance within me?

If the answer is yes, then you need to know that it will be difficult for you to live and enjoy a Spirit-filled life without fully surrendering yourself to God's will. His blessings are for those who without reserve give themselves to Him. Partial obedience is not obedience.

Am I asking God for His guidance today and the future?

In a Spirit-controlled life you can freely seek the things of God because you know that along the way every need, every dream, every hope you have is being shaped and met by God through the working of the Holy Spirit. You don't have to be frightened or ashamed to come to God. He loves you unconditionally. Therefore, the Holy Spirit has the same feelings for you. ". . . The love of God has been poured out within our hearts through the Holy Spirit who was given to us" (Romans 5:5).

> *"He who has an ear, let him hear*
> *what the Spirit says . . ."*

> *Revelation 2:7*

Our Source of Communication with God

One of the roles of the Holy Spirit is that of intercessor. He literally intercedes for us in prayer. "And in the same way the Spirit also helps our weakness; for we do not know how to pray as we should, but the Spirit Himself intercedes for us with groanings too deep for words; and He who searches the hearts knows what the mind of the Spirit is, because He intercedes for the saints according to the will of God" (Romans 8:26-27).

◆ Ask God to give you a heart that longs to know more about Him.

◆ Pray that you will be made sensitive to God's Spirit, His leading, and the ways He seeks to communicate with you. While God spoke primarily through His prophets in the Old Testament, today He speaks to the hearts and minds of those willing to seek Him.

◆ Realize that Satan will try anything to separate you from God. Refuse to yield to thoughts of condemnation, defeat, and fear. Romans 8:1 says: "There is therefore now no condemnation for those who are in Christ Jesus."

Hebrews 13:5b-6 reminds us there is no need to fear or become discouraged. Jesus is with us always. This is the promise and the role of His Spirit. " . . . for He Himself has said, 'I will never desert you, nor will I ever forsake you,' so that we confidently say, 'The Lord is my Helper, I will not be afraid.'"

"God is spirit, and those who worship Him must worship in spirit and truth."

John 4:24

Developing a Personal Relationship

God desires a personal, loving relationship with you. His acceptance of you is complete and unconditional. This doesn't mean He overlooks sin; it means you are His creation, and He is willing to go to any length to save you and then mold you into the likeness of His Son, the Lord Jesus Christ.

It's important to yield your heart to God, because when you are open to His Spirit, He makes you sensitive to His nature. Suddenly you find His loving presence a place of security and hope. During this process we begin to seek ways to know Him better and then to please Him with our life and actions.

Before His death Jesus used the word peace many times in dealing with the disciples. On one occasion He told them: "The Helper, the Holy Spirit, whom the Father will send in My name, He will teach you all things, and bring to your remembrance all that I said to you. Peace I leave with you; My peace I give to you; not as the world gives, do I give to you. Let not your heart be troubled, nor let it be fearful" (John 14:26-27).

However, the more we turn to Jesus for guidance and insight, the more we are drawn to Him in friendship. The desire for sin fades the closer we move to Him. We develop a hunger to learn more about Him, and the Spirit of God is then free to reveal Himself to us.

A lady once told me that she had been a Christian all her life and never realized that God was interested in what she did at home. She often felt as if housework and grocery shopping were mundane. Then she began to talk to God in prayer, first about the plans she had for the day and how to accomplish them. It wasn't long before she noticed her days becoming more organized. Prayers were being answered and there was a new excitement in what once was considered "household chores."

If God loves us so much, why would we fail to communicate with Him? Many complain of a lack of time, convenience, or motivation. Time alone with God is pushed to the sidelines, yet we find ourselves asking: "How can I live without Him?"

We sometimes claim it isn't convenient to pray in the morning because we have to take the children to school and get to work on time. Praying later at home is out of the question because there's too much left undone from the day — cars need to be washed, dogs walked, and supper cooked. By the time we lie down between the sheets at night our emotional and physical energies are gone and so is any thought of praying.

In the book, *The Pursuit Of God*, A.W. Tozer writes: "In our desire after God let us keep always in mind that God also has desire, and His desire is toward the sons of men, and more particularly toward those sons of men who will make the once-for-all decision to exalt Him over all. Such as these are precious to God above all treasures of earth or sea. In them God finds a theater where He can display His exceeding kindness toward us in Christ Jesus. With them God can walk unhindered; toward them He can act like the God He is."

"For the one who sows to his own flesh shall from the flesh reap corruption, but the one who sows to the Spirit shall from the Spirit reap eternal life. And let us not lose heart in doing good, for in due time we shall reap . . ."

Galatians 6:8-9

The Victory Is Yours

After the Crucifixion the disciples hid themselves for fear that they too would end up like Jesus. The place they chose to remain was in fact the last place they had been with the Lord.

There is something about returning to a place of warmth, especially after tragedy strikes, that steadies a person and provides a place of healing and hope. This was probably the case with the disciples. The upper room where they had been with Jesus the night of His arrest helped them to recall some of His greatest passages of assurance. "Do not be afraid, I will come to you." "I will not leave you comfortless; I will send another who will guide you into all wisdom and truth."

Then suddenly came the words spoken aloud to them, "Peace be with you." Their eyes lifted to see their risen Lord standing before them. He had come to them in their darkest hour just as He promised. The Holy Spirit is God's agent of love and grace. He knows all about you — your joys, sorrows, fears, defeats, and victories. He knows your desires and works continuously to shape them after God's will.

"Now the Lord is the Spirit, and where the Spirit of the Lord is, there is freedom."

2 Corinthians 3:17 (NIV)

One of the last appearances Jesus made to His disciples was along the Sea of Galilee. Some scholars note that several members of the group had returned to their former occupations. If this is true, then it explains why Peter, John, and Andrew had returned to fishing. Once they recognized the Lord, they immediately headed the boat back to shore. After a meal of grilled fish, Jesus took Peter aside to talk about what had happened the night of His arrest.

Merrill Tenney explains: "The disciples were no doubt aware of Peter's denial of Jesus, and the commission that Jesus renewed with him in their presence would reassure them of Peter's place among them. . . ." However, the chief reason for this narrative was "to let Peter know that the Lord still loved him and has not cast him out."

Each of us at one time or the other has done something to cast a shadow over our relationship with the Lord. We struggle and seek forgiveness and long to know that "the Lord still loves us and has not cast us out." Not only does God's Spirit empower us for ministry, but He also brings restoration, comfort, and healing when we have fallen prey to sin or some trial. God has not left us comfortless. He has provided a strong, unshakable Source of hope through His Holy Spirit, but it's our responsibility to ask for His help and empowerment.

As you go through your day-to-day routine, ask yourself, "How much of myself am I making available to God? How much of my life is Spirit-controlled versus self-indulgent? Be honest, remembering that God has one goal in mind, and that is to bring you into a close, personal relationship with His Son.

We can praise Him that through Jesus Christ our sins are forgiven and our relationship restored to our heavenly Father. A good way to increase your awareness of the Holy Spirit is to begin each day with a commitment to walk in the Spirit. Pray that the fruit of the Spirit would be evident to those around you: ". . . love, joy, peace, patience, kindness, goodness, faithfulness, gentleness, [and] self-control" (Galatians 5:22-23).

When aggravations come, remember that a mind set on the things of the Spirit results in a life and of peace. If you think negatively and brood over life's troubles, chances are you will feel stress and lack true peace. The apostle Paul wrote that the mind of the flesh is set on the things of the flesh, and each of us knows where this philosophy eventually ends up.

Do you spend time thinking through and praying for your day? Anticipate any problems and ask God to show you the way to handle each detail. Then claim His victory as you seek the guidance of His Holy Spirit. Faith is the catalyst for the release of the dynamic power of the Spirit in your life.

By following this simple pattern you will begin to notice that the Holy Spirit is rapidly becoming an important part of your walk with Jesus Christ. As I said in the concluding chapter of *The Wonderful Spirit-Filled Life*: "The Holy Spirit will become as important to you as you allow Him to be. He won't force Himself on you. He sits back quietly and waits. Give Him control. He's not asking for rededication. He's asking for surrender."

It's only after you have declared your inadequacy that He can come to your assistance. As long as you try to "make life work" your way or "force an issue" into being, He is unable to accomplish the task He has been given to do.

Only through true surrender can you know and experience the fullness of God's loving intent for your life. Don't miss the very best God has for you. He is waiting even now to bring light to your darkness, hope to situations of disillusionment, and victory over defeat. Trust Him and ask Him to lead you into all truth through the power of His Holy Spirit.

THE POWER OF PRAYER

One of my earliest memories as a young child is my mother praying. My father died when I was a baby, so she had to work long hours to support us. Every day she was on her knees thanking God for what He gave us and asking Him to meet our needs. She would say to me: "Son, let's take our problems to the Lord."

Even though finances were tight, and sometimes it looked like ends would not meet, we never went without. Always at just the right time, God would send what we required. But her prayers taught me more than how God takes care of us. She showed me that God is real — someone who listens and loves and is involved in the lives of His children. Prayer was talking to a God who never got tired of hearing and never misunderstood.

At the heart of my mother's time with God was communication, the basis and building block of any relationship. Think about how important communication is with people you are close to. Without it, you can forget about intimacy or unity or mutual enjoyment. In fact, you could say that without communication, you have little more than a casual acquaintance.

Imagine that you make a new friend and you can't wait to get to know this person. There is one problem, however — you never speak. Whenever you meet, you both just sit quietly and look at each other in admiring silence. How long could you go on like this? If you ever want to have meaningful interaction, you *must* communicate.

The same is true in developing your relationship with God after you have accepted His Son, Jesus Christ, as your Savior. If you don't ever talk to Him and listen to what He is saying to you, you miss out on the joy of close fellowship and learning more about His character and His love. When you do talk to Him and open your heart to His response, you discover direction and fulfillment that transcends the limitations of human relationships.

Maybe you have never thought about prayer as a two-way communication process before. In your childhood, prayer was merely a bedtime excercise with little personal meaning, and now as an adult you still do not understand its significance. Prayer seems to be something the pastor does on Sunday morning, not an activity designed for you as an individual.

Or maybe you do understand the purpose of prayer, and you have enjoyed it as part of your walk with the Lord for a while. But there are times when prayer is not the dynamic part of your life that you know it can be. Perhaps you did not receive the answer you wanted, or you are not sure if you got an answer at all. You are not confident that you know how to pray, or how to know what God is saying to you in return.

You're not alone, and it's never too late to begin. Don't let anyone tell you that prayer is only for those who have had a relationship with God for a long time. Prayer is for *you* right where you are today.

Why Should I Pray?

As I mentioned already, the primary reason is one of relationship. Prayer is essentially a conversation with God in which you praise Him, thank Him for His blessings, and tell Him what is on your heart and mind. In the process, God speaks to you through His Word, by the Holy Spirit, and others — a pastor or trusted Christian friend.

God commands you to pray. Philippians 4:6-7 says, "Be anxious for nothing, but in everything by prayer and supplication with thanksgiving let your requests be made known to God. And the peace of God, which surpasses all comprehension, shall guard your hearts and your minds in Christ Jesus."

Prayer is not a burdensome responsibility for the believer; it is a joy and privilege. Each day, you can talk to the God who created everything in existence. He is all-powerful and all-knowing. Nothing can remove you from His loving presence, and He wants you to share every aspect of your existence with Him (Psalm 139:1-10; Romans 8:35).

Prayer gives you the proper understanding of your position as God's child and an awareness of His involvement in your life. When you bring Him your problems, cares, and anxieties, what you are acknowledging is this: "God, I need You. I don't have the answers, but I know You do." This is an expression of total dependence on Him, and it is humbling. But recognizing the Lord's power and sufficiency in all things is key to experiencing His security and abundant provision.

What Should I Say When I Pray?

Related to this question are other ones such as, "Is there a wrong way to pray?" or "Do I need to say the Lord's Prayer every time?" These are not trivial issues in any way; in fact, if these are your concerns, you show that you are aware how awesome and wonderful prayer really is.

No, there is not a "wrong" way to pray in the sense that you must worry about saying the wrong thing, or using the wrong words. God understands what you are thinking and feeling; He knows exactly what you mean (Psalm 139:3-4). Furthermore, the Holy Spirit, who lives in you the moment you accept Jesus as your Savior, is continually praying on your behalf.

"And in the same way the Spirit also helps our weakness; for we do not know how to pray as we should, but the Spirit Himself intercedes for us with groanings too deep for words; and He who searches the hearts knows what the mind of the Spirit is, because He intercedes for the saints according to the will of God" (Romans 8:26-27).

What God does consider essential is our *attitude* in prayer. It is crucial to remember that God's ultimate goal is not simply to be a storehouse who grants wishes and desires; instead, His purpose is fellowship, love, and communion. Of course, He wants to bless you with good things, even beyond your wildest imaginations (1 Corinthians 2:9; Ephesians 3:20). But you are not to approach Him as a spoiled or ungrateful child who doesn't have love blended with proper respect.

In her book *Seeking God*, Joni Eareckson Tada says: "So why do we often pray so carelessly, even sloppily? Take a look at the Old Testament. The priests who approached God had an attitude of holy carefulness. . . . Our prayers are spiritual sacrifices too. . . . Yes, God is happy and willing to hear each of our requests. But the Bible tells us that we are to 'worship God acceptably with reverence and awe, for our God is a consuming fire'

(Hebrews 12:28-29). . . . Then we have an attitude of submission, of humility, of deference to the King of kings and Lord of lords."

Does having respect mean you can't be honest about your feelings? Absolutely not. For moving examples of emotion-packed prayers, turn to the Psalms. King David felt anger, impatience, weariness, loneliness, fear; and he never hesitated to tell God the truth. He knew that God wanted him to pour out his heart — all of it, not just the "acceptable" parts (Psalm 62:8). But David always recognized the power and holiness of his Lord and responded with a willing, worshipful, and repentant spirit.

When Should I Pray?

Many believers, even when they recognize the importance of praying, feel that they don't pray often enough. They pray when they are in trouble or have a pressing need, but when the pressure slacks off, so does their diligence in prayer.

It is a typical scenario; pain or hardship drives us to our knees in a hurry, but somehow in peaceful times the motivation to come before Him wanes. The apostle Paul addressed this tendency in his letter to the Thessalonians, who were struggling hard against the worldly influences around them.

"Rejoice always; *pray without ceasing*; in

everything give thanks; for this is God's will for you in Christ Jesus" (1 Thessalonians 5:16-18, emphasis mine). What does it mean to pray without ceasing? Does he mean that you must be voicing a prayer out loud or in your head every waking moment? No, of course not, but don't miss what Paul is saying. The point here is priority; time with God in prayer should be number one — first place in your heart and mind. Nothing else comes before spending time with Him.

Jesus made it clear that prayer is the most important part of fellowship with God. When He was on this earth, He spent much time alone talking with the Father (Luke 5:16). The crowds thronged around Him; the disciples needed His attention. Yet even with all the demands of His time and physical energy, He made communing with God His foremost activity.

Nineteenth-century pastor and evangelist E.M. Bounds explains: "Prayer was the secret of [Jesus'] power, the law of His life, the inspiration of His toil and the source of His wealth, His joy, His communion and His strength. . . . His campaigns were arranged and His victories were gained in the struggles . . . of His all night praying."

Colossians 4:2 says: "Devote yourselves to prayer, keeping alert in it with an attitude of thanksgiving." The word *devote* has a much stronger definition in the original Greek. Literally, it means constant attention and perseverance, a continual process.

As you go through the day, lift up the needs and problems you encounter. If a task goes well, thank Him for His help. If you are on your way to a meeting, ask Him to prepare your mind and give you clarity and insight. Share with Him all of your experiences and learn to rely on His guidance. Ephesians 5:19 reminds us that we are to go about "speaking to one another in psalms and hymns and spiritual songs, singing and making melody with your heart to the Lord." Prayer is more than just an activity; it is to be a continual mind-set and all-pervasive attitude.

How Do I Make Prayer a Regular Part of My Life?

Few things are more frustrating than knowing how vital prayer is and then not following through. We have all struggled in this area of commitment, but until we join the Lord in heaven, we must continue actively to seek out communication with Him.

Maybe you started a specific "prayer plan" before. You made a commitment to spend a certain number of minutes praying every day, and for a while, you were faithful to that resolution. As weeks passed, however, you probably skipped a day or two. The phone rang just as you sat down, or the kids came home early from school, or you remembered another obligation.

Whatever the reason, the day slipped by without quality time with your Savior. There are some practical ways to combat the clamor of the day and find consistent victory and joy in prayer. First, you need to *set a specific time*. Make an "appointment" with the Lord and even write it down on your schedule for the day. When prayer is a planned event, you can take the steps necessary to protect that time.

Be careful, though, not to fall into a mechanized mind-set because you put prayer on a list. Don't feel that it is just another part of the routine or another chore to check off. Remember that you are making arrangements for a special encounter with Almighty God, and over time, your excitement builds as you learn to anticipate those fulfilling moments.

Next, *locate a private place*. What is so important about a particular spot? You can pray anywhere (and anytime); but when you select one location, it becomes a personal sanctuary. That place can be a special room or nook or closet or chair in the corner — wherever you are the most free from avoidable distractions.

Write your prayers in a journal or notebook. Put the date at the end of each one; and when God answers, draw a single line through the request so you can still read it. Record the answer date at the end of the line, and as you review the pages, you can rejoice at His provision. You will say, "God loves me. He is interested in me. I am growing in my faith, and He is actively involved in my life." The excitement of this review process is unbeatable.

What Does Jesus Mean When He Says "Ask, and It Shall Be Given to You"? Will He Give Me Everything I Ask For?

This is what Jesus said to His disciples on the hillside as part of the Sermon on the Mount: "Ask, and it shall be given to you; seek, and you shall find; knock, and it shall be opened to you. For everyone who asks receives, and he who seeks finds, and to him who knocks it shall be opened.

"Or what man is there among you, when his son shall ask him for a loaf, will give him a stone? Or if he shall ask for a fish, he will not give him a snake, will he? If you then, being evil, know how to give good gifts to your children, how much more shall your Father who is in heaven give what is good to those who ask Him!" (Matthew 7:7-11)

Maybe you asked God for something with all your heart, and you feel that He did not answer you. It was the greatest desire you ever had, you trusted Him with it, but you heard nothing. Disappointment set in, and for a while now praying has become a chore. When you read this passage about the certainty of answered prayer, you wrestle with a little hurt and anger. You wonder, *Why doesn't God do it for me?*

Let's look more closely at how Jesus describes the process of interacting with your heavenly Father. First, it's important to remember that prayer is not passive; it is active involvement in a relationship to the living God who wants to bless you.

That thought is so vital to understanding what happens in prayer. I'll say it again — *He wants to bless you*. In every way, He has your best interest at heart (Psalm 37:4). He is superior to any earthly father; there is not one bit of selfishness, indecision, or ignorance in His actions towards you. How do we know this? Jesus Christ proved it at Calvary. When He laid down His life in your place, He said, "You are worth everything to Me."

When Jesus commands you to ask, He is encouraging you to pray and take every concern to Him. But He wants you involved with the answer every step of the way. Notice the progression here. You begin with simple asking, telling God what you want or need and placing the desire in His care.

Then you move to the seeking and knocking phase, looking for His answer in the opportunities He brings. At times, all God wants you to do is ask, especially in heartbreak and tragedy. You're helpless, and He wants you to be quiet and still before Him (Psalms 37:7; 46:10). But these moments are the exception to the rule.

For example, you ask Him to give you a deeper comprehension of His Word. He does this, yes, but *you* have to open your Bible and take the initiative of disciplined study. The high school student going off to college who asks God to reveal the right school must do some active looking around — getting catalogs, making phone calls, gathering information. The Lord wants you to participate in His provision and look for His direction.

Proverbs 3:5-6 gives this comforting promise: "Trust in the Lord with all your heart, and do not lean on your own understanding. In all your ways acknowledge Him, and He will make your paths straight." He never lets you wander in confusion and frustration when you ask Him to show the way; He intends for you to live in the security of His clear and affirming direction (1 Corinthians 14:33).

Be assured of this: there is no such thing as unanswered prayer; God answers every prayer from His children. He responds with either a *yes*, a *no*, or a *wait*. What most people mean when they refer to unanswered prayer is a request that God has answered *no*. Sometimes it does not seem like a "real" answer when God doesn't respond in the way you hope or expect, but what He says is the absolute best for you.

What Does It Mean When God Answers No to My Request?

Look again at verse 11 of Matthew 7. Since you know that God loves you perfectly, you have the confidence that His withholding something from you is a positive, not a negative. God never says no for spite! He always has a reason.

His refusal is a call for you to inspect two things closely — your heart and your request. Before you begin the examination, though, be honest about how you feel regarding His answer. If you are hurt and disappointed, say so. If you are angry, tell Him. He will show you why He denied what you want. To aid in discerning His purposes, ask yourself the following questions.

How Is My Relationship with the Lord?

Psalm 66:18 says: "If I regard wickedness in my heart, the Lord will not hear." Don't be discouraged when you hear this verse and wonder how God could ever listen to what you say. God does not shut off His blessing every time you sin or make a mistake — certainly not. But any unconfessed sin in your life hinders your fellowship with God. If you feel conviction or heaviness about a certain action or issue, deal with it immediately and put aside any barrier to open and free communication.

Is My Prayer Specific?

When you pray vague or indefinite prayers, you show that the request does not mean very much to you. Otherwise, you would take the time to think it through and verbalize the details. Anything less is like going into a restaurant and ordering "food and drink." You need to state the desires of your heart with exactness so you will know when God has answered and so He receives the glory.

Catherine Marshall explains in her book *Adventures in Prayer*: "God insists that we ask, not because *He* needs to know our situation, but because *we* need the spiritual discipline of asking. Similarly, making our requests specific forces us to take a step forward in faith. The reason many of us retreat into vague generalities when we pray is not because we think too highly of God, but because we think too little. If we pray for something definite and our request is not granted, we fear to lose the little faith we had. So we fall back on the safe route of highly 'spiritual' prayers — the kind that Jesus brushed aside as not true prayer at all, just self-deceptive 'talking to ourselves.'"

Is the Request in Keeping with the Character of Christ?

In other words, is it a prayer that Jesus might have prayed? Think through your motivations and ask the Lord to reveal your true intentions. Selfishness, pride, wrongful ambition — check to see that no other purposes are polluting your petitions. James 4:3 says: "You ask and do not receive, because you ask with wrong motives, so that you may spend it on your pleasures." The *why* of your prayers is as important as the *what*.

Do I Really Believe God Will Answer Me?

Doubt and prayer don't mix at all. If you approach the Lord worried that He does not hear or will ignore you, you become like the faithless one described in James 1:5-8, double-minded and unstable in all your ways. When you worry and waver, you essentially undermine the peace God plans for you to have. "Without faith it is impossible to please Him, for he who comes to God must believe that He is, and that He is a rewarder of those who seek Him" (Hebrews 11:6). Pray in joyful expectation of His reply.

The most intense time of emotional trial may come after you have completed this personal search. Many times you are not harboring unconfessed sin; your life and your desires line up with His truth. What are you supposed to think then?

Max Lucado puts the situation into perspective in his book *In the Eye of the Storm*. "A day with a car full of kids will teach you a lot about God. Transporting a family from one city to another is closely akin to God transporting us from our home to His. And some of life's stormiest hours occur when the passenger and the Driver disagree on the destination. . . .

"Can you imagine the outcome if a parent honored each request of each child during a trip? We'd inch our bloated bellies from one ice-cream store to the next. . . . Can you imagine the chaos if a parent indulged every indulgence? Can you imagine if God indulged each of ours? *No* is a necessary word to take on a trip. Destination has to reign over Dairy Deluxe Ice Cream Sundae. . . .

"Note God's destiny for your life. Salvation. . . . His itinerary includes stops that encourage your journey. He frowns on stops that deter you. When His sovereign plan and your earthly plan collide, a decision must be made. Who's in charge of this journey? . . . The requests my children made on the road to Grandma's weren't evil. They weren't unfair. . . . But most of the requests were unnecessary. My four-year-old daughter would argue that fact. From her viewpoint, another soft drink is indispensable to her happiness. I know otherwise, so I say no."

God wants you to seek Him more than you seek answers to your prayers. Sometimes, especially when God says no, it is easy to become absorbed in desiring the gift rather than adoring the Giver. The key to maintaining spiritual balance is focusing on God's ultimate goal — conforming you to the image of His Son, Jesus Christ (Colossians 3:10).

The Lord may withhold what you ask for in order to teach you to trust Him. Think about what would happen if He granted every request the moment you asked. Most likely you would begin to take Him for granted and not value His responses. God wants to build your faith by making you hold on to His promises when circumstances seem impossible. To cease praying and trusting is to give more credit to your own understanding than to God's infinite wisdom. He wants you to persist in prayer and ignore your feelings, in spite of what you see. Over time, as you allow Him to prove Himself faithful, you find it easier to trust Him.

In some cases, He is preparing you for what He has in store. You may not be ready emotionally, spiritually, or physically for His answer and He wants you to develop a little more. Or perhaps He simply has something far better in mind, greater than what you asked or hoped for.

Mary and Martha prayed earnestly that

Jesus would come and heal their dear, dying brother Lazarus. (John 11) Not only did Jesus not come before Lazarus died, but Lazarus was in his grave four days before Jesus arrived in Bethany. Listen to the anguish and confusion in Martha's voice, wondering why Jesus did not come: "Lord, if You had been here, my brother would not have died" (v. 21).

She knew the truth; Jesus *could have* healed Lazarus if He had chosen to. In fact, Jesus did not even need to be there to do it. He could have spoken the word, and Lazarus would have walked away a well man. But Jesus said no. Why? He had bigger plans that would bring God even more glory than they imagined. Jesus raised Lazarus from the dead, and as a result, many placed their faith in Jesus.

Above all else, the Lord works in ways that will bring Him praise and point those around you to Him. When you seek His face and thank Him for His goodness to you in all things, He reveals His perfect design when the time is right.

How Should I Pray for Other People?

When you are praying for yourself, you usually know just how to express what you want and how you feel. But when you pray for someone else, it's much more difficult to concentrate and articulate requests for them. After all, you are not intimately familiar with their most personal needs and desires.

Do you ever tell someone you will pray for him and then forget? You run into him a week or so later and privately hope he won't ask if you have been praying for him. Realizing the place that prayer has in dynamic Christian fellowship is a tremendous help. God designed prayer as the primary means for caring for our brothers and sisters in Christ. It's God's support network for His children, and He calls every one of us to active, concerned intercession for others.

"I [Paul] urge, then, first of all, that requests, prayers, intercession and thanksgiving be made for everyone — for kings and all those in authority, that we may live peaceful and quiet lives in all godliness and holiness. This is good, and pleases God our Savior, who wants all men to be saved and to come to a knowledge of the truth. . . . I want men everywhere to lift up holy hands in prayer, without anger or disputing" (1 Timothy 2:1-8, NIV).

Whether you pray for neighbors, coworkers, or elected officials, realize that your prayers are the link between their needs and God's blessings in their lives. Of course, God does not *need* your prayers in order to work in their behalf, but He chooses to involve you so you can experience the joy of His benefits to those around you.

Where do you begin? You start with a heart

of love and compassion and a desire to see
God change the person's life in some way.
Next, you must identify with the need; you
must feel what the other person feels as much
as possible. When Jesus looked out over the
needy crowds, His heart was moved with
compassion (Matthew 20:34; Luke 7:13).

Most important, you must be willing to be
involved in the answer, to "get your hands
dirty" working with them if that is what God
calls you to do. God's answer for them may
include something only you can offer. As you
pray with perseverence for ones God brings to
your attention, you will see His blessings
unfold mightily.

PART II
Follow Me

GROWING
IN FAITH

If you have ever visited a museum or special historical exhibit, you probably saw pictures and paintings of famous people from the past who did great things for the world and for society. There they are, with a nameplate or plaque describing what they did, for generations of onlookers to appreciate and remember.

Try to imagine the display if the great heroes of faith from the Bible had a special place in a museum. You would see a picture of Noah, building an ark just because God told him to, in spite of the mocking onlookers. You'd see the image of Moses, lifting up his staff and stretching out his hand over the Red Sea, so that God would part the waters for the fleeing Israelites. Joseph would be on the wall too the one who trusted God to deliver him after his brothers sold him into slavery as a young man.

The portrait of Samson would show him pushing down the pillars of the Philistine house, when God gave him back his strength. The Prophet Elijah would be in the middle of his dramatic showdown with the prophets of Baal. Ruth's picture would capture the moment when she told her mother-in-law Naomi she would follow her God and stay by her side. King David's picture would show a young boy standing before the mighty, taunting giant Goliath.

The Apostle Peter would be standing in astonishment before the living Savior, exclaiming, "You are the Christ." And the picture of Stephen, the first believer to be martyred for his faith in Jesus, would highlight his gaze upward to heaven as the stones flew at his body.

Now try to imagine another picture next to all of these. It is down the hallway quite a bit farther, because the walls are filled up with people of faith of many years. It has the same kind of frame and a plaque with words underneath it. As you look closer, you realize you recognize the person in the portrait — it is you.

If you are startled at the thought that your picture could be hanging in the "hall of faith," you shouldn't be. You demonstrated faith the moment you trusted Jesus Christ to be your Savior and cleanse you from sin. You weren't relying on your own resources to try to please God, by attempting to work your way into His favor. In that time of humility and repentance before Him in prayer, you acknowledged that Christ and Christ alone was sufficient. You needed Jesus in order to have an eternal relationship with God, and by trusting Him for forgiveness, you took an incredible step of faith — faith that God gave you to enable you to trust Him with your soul and eternal destiny.

So What Is It?

It would probably be more helpful to begin with a brief description of what faith is not, given that there are many false definitions that can cause confusion.

Faith isn't just something for spiritual heroes or those of great renown. It is not a mysterious condition that "happens" to you. It is not a forced emotional or mental state or a contrived mind-set that admits only "positive thinking." Faith doesn't depend on your ability to manufacture feelings of confidence or joy. Faith isn't something that you need "more of" before you develop your relationship with the Lord. Faith isn't something that "impresses" God and therefore moves Him to do something for you.

Put very simply, faith is basic trust that God is who He says He is and that He will do what He promises in His Word. It may sound like too basic an explanation, but that is the heart of what it means to have faith in God. The following illustration has often been used to illustrate the difference between intellectual trust and real trust, or faith.

When you see a chair that looks sturdy, you have no problem sitting in it. As you place your weight on the seat and actually sit in the chair, you are essentially *trusting* that chair with your body. If you only *say* that the chair can hold you, but you never sit in it, you are not trusting yourself to the care of that chair. Though this comparison is limited in many respects, you could say that faith is believing the chair will support you at the same time that you physically let it support you.

God's Word gives His definition of faith. Hebrews 11:1 says, "Now faith is the assurance of things hoped for, the conviction of things not seen." Even though you cannot perceive spiritual truths with your physical senses, you know within your spirit that they are real because God says they are. God takes your trust in Him and grows it, nurturing it day by day. As time passes and you enjoy an intimate relationship with the Lord, and as you see how He operates in your daily life, your trust in Him and His faithfulness to you solidifies.

This process is often referred to as a strengthening of your faith. Through a living experience of fellowship with God, you come to depend and rely on Him with your entire being. That is genuine faith, and that is what motivated the great characters of the Bible. If faith depended on how much we could give to God, then no one would have faith. Moses didn't stand before the Pharaoh of Egypt because he believed he would perform well for God. He stood up and spoke before Pharaoh because God gave him the power and ability.

When you read the stories of Old Testament heroes, you discover that many were powerless or poor or unskilled when God laid His hand on their lives. They became His instruments to do mighty works as they trusted Him to do the job; they were weak people with a strong God.

Why Should I Trust God?

When you follow any kind of leader, one of your first concerns is that person's trustworthiness. A leader who vacillates randomly in making decisions or who in general demonstrates poor character is not someone you feel comfortable following. If you are going to walk side by side with someone and pursue his goals as your own, then that person must be worthy of such trust.

Human leaders always fall short of the ideal, but God never does. He is holy, righteous, omnipotent, omniscient, eternal, and perfectly loving. First Timothy 6:15-16 describes the Lord this way: "God, the blessed and only Ruler, the King of kings and Lord of lords, who alone is immortal and who lives in unapproachable light, whom no one has seen or can see." (NIV)

The God who created the entire universe out of nothing fashioned you personally. You are custom-made. He loves you unconditionally and has a plan for you, one that is good and satisfying and glorifying to Him (Psalm 139). You can trust Him with your life because He is your Maker. When you rest in His love and trust Him to do His work through you, you feel a significance and self-worth that cannot be taken away, and at the same time you become a channel of His blessing to others.

Have you ever had to take your car to a repair shop? Then you understand how it feels to wait for the mechanic to call and tell you what is wrong. Suppose when the call comes, the technician says that you need new brakes and a general tune-up.

At this point, you have to make a choice. You may either rely on the mechanic's word and have the work done, or you can take your car home. In most cases, you are probably going to have the repairs made. Why? You understand that the adjustments are for the benefit of the automobile. Without them, the car won't be able to operate at top efficiency, and it could be unsafe.

When God looks at your life, which He is carefully nurturing, He sees every detail with absolute precision. An auto mechanic can be in error about a car, but God is never wrong when it comes to knowing what is best for you. In all things He is working to conform you to the image of Jesus Christ and to prepare you for good works (Ephesians 2:10).

This character-building and guidance system are part of a step-by-step, gradual process. Along the way, God makes adjustments, either to keep you on track or to steer you in new directions. These changes might be minor, or they could be big and momentous. For example, the Lord could ask you to get rid of a personal habit or He might call you to change your entire career.

When the disciples were laboring with their nets at the Sea of Galilee, Peter and James and John had no concept of all the things that Jesus had in store for them. "[Jesus] saw two brothers, Simon who was called Peter, and Andrew his brother, casting a net into the sea; for they were fishermen. And He said to them, 'Follow Me, and I will make you fishers of men.' And they immediately left the nets, and followed Him." (Matthew 4:18-20)

No one knows for certain, but historical evidence and scriptural context tell us that these men were probably brought up in good Jewish homes. They had learned God's laws and heard His Word, but this was God as they had never known Him before. They could not anticipate the blessings and trials of the future, but they did know one thing: Jesus Christ was calling them to follow Him. And they obeyed.

As you mature in Christ, you discover one of your greatest difficulties is putting His instructions into practice. Whenever you sense

God directing you to make an adjustment to fit His purposes, you experience a critical turning point. Very often, God furnishes only what you need to know in order to make a decision. The future may appear fuzzy or incomprehensible from a human perspective, but He is not calling you to grasp the breadth and depth of His infinite wisdom. God wants you to trust Him completely and take the simple steps of obedience that He sets before you.

An All-Terrain Faith

If you have ever seen one of the new "all-terrain vehicles" that are so popular today, you were probably impressed with the tires. They are rugged and tough, and have treads that can grip any surface, from smooth asphalt to the grittiest of off-road trails. The tires are part of what make these vehicles so versatile; they can go anywhere they need to go because they are equipped with the right gear.

When you trust God to take care of you, you can be assured that He will equip you for the challenge. Circumstances that seem painful and confusing do not throw you off His chosen path because you know the Lord always uses the hurt to work out His special purposes in your life. In his book *Trusting God,* Jerry Bridges points out some of the spiritual problems that believers encounter when they go through a "smooth road" time:

"As difficult as it is to trust God in times of adversity, there are other times when it may be even more difficult to trust Him. These would be times when circumstances are going well, when, to use David's expression, 'The boundary lines have fallen . . . in pleasant places' (Psalm 16:6). During times of temporal blessings and prosperity, we are prone to put our trust in those blessings, or even worse, in ourselves as the providers of those blessings.

"During times of prosperity and favorable circumstances, we show our trust in God by acknowledging Him as the provider of all those blessings. . . . Soloman said, 'When times are good, be happy; but when times are bad, consider: God has made the one as well as the other' (Ecclesiastes 7:14). God makes the good times as well as the bad times. In adversity we tend to doubt God's fatherly care, but in prosperity we tend to forget it. If we are to trust God, we must acknowledge our dependence upon Him at all times. . . ."

Facing Life's Unknowns

Whenever circumstances change suddenly, especially when they change for what we perceive to be the worse, the shift may cause us to question where we're going. Whether you've been a believer for one month or one decade, it is easy to struggle with thoughts of doubt. Once again, this is the place where trust becomes the issue. The more "unex-

plainable" situations that you move through
and then see God's provision as part of the
larger picture, the less difficult it is to trust
Him for the next crisis or heartache. This next
story is a riveting example of something
frightening and unknown turning into a reason for a lifetime of rejoicing.

As the pains of childbirth subsided, the
woman held her new baby boy in her arms for
the first time. She should have felt joy, but
instead she felt a sickening knot forming in
her heart.

She knew what the government had
ordered her to do. The law said her baby boy
must be killed immediately, just because he
was a boy. But she also knew what Almighty
God wanted her to do. Under the threat of
death if she disobeyed, this mother made a
decision. She said no to the evil law and yes to
the Lord.

How was the woman Jochebed to know
that one day God would use her boy Moses to
deliver an entire nation out of Egyptian
oppression? How could she possibly understand the eternal consequences of one action
of faith? All she saw was a single choice, but
because she perceived this trial through the
eyes of faith, God turned defeat into hope for
countless generations.

Maybe your life is peaceful, tranquil, and

predictable right now. You might even struggle with a little boredom or lack of motivation, since things are so mundane. You are reveling in a time of rest. But have you thought ahead to how you will react if bad news comes?

Let's say you're sitting around the house chatting with a next-door neighbor when the phone rings. The words you hear leave you stunned and speechless. You gasp. Your friend rushes to your side and says with a panicked voice, "What's wrong?" In one instant, the familiar, comfortable world you once took for granted feels blown to pieces, and you don't think those pieces will ever fit together again.

This scenario isn't presented to scare you or intimidate you into fear and anxiety about the future, but it is intended to help you consider the importance of absolute trust in God. Nothing is beyond His control. Nothing takes Him by surprise. And He promises to take the vilest situation and the most bitter tragedy and turn it into good for you. You can never read or meditate on the promise of Romans 8:28 too many times: "And we know that God causes all things to work together for good to those who love God, to those who are called according to His purpose."

Those who have not accepted Jesus as their Savior don't have a valid reason to "look on the bright side." The substance of our faith, the reality of our hope, is a living Savior who shed His blood to redeem you and give you an abundant life that begins now, in this life (John 10:10). Hebrews 6:19-20 says: "This hope we have as an anchor of the soul, a hope both sure and steadfast and one which enters within the veil [of God's presence], where Jesus has entered as a forerunner for us."

Faith Means Obedience

Almost eighty years after his mother Jochebed hid him from Pharaoh's men, a moment of decision came for Moses. He was out in the desert tending the family's sheep as he would on any other ordinary day. Then suddenly, he saw flames shooting upward, engulfing a bush without even singeing a single twig. It was not difficult for Moses to understand immediately that this scene was radically different from any one he had encountered before. Then in another moment of awe, God spoke from the fire.

God said: "Therefore, come now, and I will send you to Pharaoh, so that you may bring My people, the sons of Israel, out of Egypt" (Ex. 3:10). When Moses asked God what he should call Him, God replied, "I Am Who I Am" (v. 14).

God identified Himself as the eternal God who has no beginning or end. His character does not change. His purposes stand forever.

God was saying to Moses: "I am all-powerful, sovereign, and all-wise. I can take care of every problem. I have a plan. If you obey Me, you will find joy and fulfillment beyond imagination."

After the promises of God and the testimony of the past, wouldn't you think that Moses would have responded with a resounding "Yes, Lord!" His answer to God was less than enthusiastic: "What if they will not believe me, or listen to what I say?" (Ex. 4:1) Moses was filled with self-doubt and needless fear.

Have you ever been reluctant to trust God with confident faith, even though you know that He is able to do anything? Moses struggled with God for quite a while on this very issue. Finally, after the Lord countered every protest and refusal, Moses obeyed.

Look closely at what occurred when Moses recognized God's control over his life: he had a clearly defined mission and a reason for living. No matter what happened — and Moses would soon experience a lot of grief at the hands of an angry Pharaoh — he knew that God would see him through.

You can depend on the same absolute security as you submit your heart to the Lord. When you do yield to Him in faith, be prepared for some mighty transformations. You won't stay the same person for long; you'll become a person who sees life through the eyes of faith.

◆ *You view trials as opportunities.*

Before Moses know what God was up to, his long years in the desert as a fugitive from Egyptian law seemed a waste of valuable time. Yet when he glimpsed the future from God's perspective, the purpose became clear. During his desert years, God had quietly built into him solid leadership qualities, and the physical hardships gave him survival skills he would use later on the flight out of Egypt.

◆ *You desire obedience more than you want power or material wealth.*

Moses led a pampered life as the adopted son of the Pharaoh; it would have been easy for him to opt for a permanent life of ease rather than to take up the burdens of an oppressed people. You can learn the same lesson Moses did — it is not worth compromising and disobeying on "small" issues in order to secure money or avoid criticism from peers.

◆ *You see all of life in God's presence.*

All events are a part of God's blessing. The good and the bad play a role in His perfect pattern. Nothing can ruin your future. Your sure destination is the reason you do not have to give in to the deceit of feelings of despair or hopelessness.

When Moses' life was through, he had the joy of the knowledge that he came out a winner for one reason: he trusted God. Like all of us, he had times of questioning and anger and grumbling, but he learned the power of faith in the living God.

Moses was a risktaker, the kind God calls you to be in your walk with Him. In the book *Telling Yourself The Truth,* William Backus and Marie Chapian explain: "Faith itself is a risk. You must trust God and act in faith in order to take that step that you cannot see. If you're going to walk on water, you need to be willing to *take the chance* that you might sink to the bottom. . . .

"The misbelief that it is stupid or sinful to make decisions which might turn out wrong is unfounded. We're told to be wise as serpents, harmless as doves. Wisdom does not mean acting in fear or cowardice.

"Perfect love casts out fear means to us that the love of God has wiped out the power of fear over our lives if we will use God's methods of conquering it. 'Cast your fears [cares] on Me!' He explains. 'Give them to Me! I know what to do with them.' It is in this way that we are set free to take risks.

"Then whether we succeed or fail is not our utmost concern. We are not enslaved by fear of negative results. We willingly allow

ourselves possible failure, possible negative
results. . . .

"The Christian walking by the Spirit, in the
will of God, can trust that outcomes of his
actions in faith are totally in the hands of the
Father. The truth for the Christian is that disaster, catastrophe, or utter defeat *cannot
occur.* We have no business thinking in those
terms! *God never fails.*"

Faith and Setting Goals

Some believers live in bondage to the idea
that they cannot make decisions or plan ahead
or look forward to the future because they do
not know for certain what God has in store
for them. The good news is that is not the
way God designed faith to operate. God
instilled within you the desire to work and
plan and be forward-thinking; He wants you
to anticipate His good plans for tomorrow.

Have you ever watched students in a graduation ceremony? You can see the thrilled
expressions on their faces because they worked
so diligently to get their diplomas. When the
march is over, they shout for joy, leap up and
down, and talk with eagerness together about
where they are headed now.

That is how it feels to accomplish what you
set out to do, and this feeling is wholesome.
As a special workmanship in Christ, you are a
new creation full of worth and potential

(Psalm 30:5; 2 Corinthians 5:17). God wants you to set specific goals based on His principles and to reach them through the strength He provides.

Goals are really a natural outgrowth of godly priorities, the things on which you place the most value. Your first activity in setting up a list of Christ-centered goals is to ensure that your priorities line up with God's. Matthew 6:33 says: "Seek first His kingdom and His righteousness; and all these things shall be added to you." God promises to fill your life with abundance as you learn to love Him first.

When your value system is confronted by the truth of Matthew 6:33, you are on the positive road to a godly understanding of what it means to have faith in God and set personal goals that fit His purposes. Ask yourself the following question: What does the Lord want me to do in the area of _____? You can fill in the blank with issues such as family life, finances, spiritual growth, the list is endless.

After you itemize the areas in which you feel God is leading you to take action, you're ready to build the kind of motivation that keeps you focused and on target. Writing down objectives is often helpful. In order to determine if your goals fit your walk of faith, submit the objectives on your list to the following criteria.

◆ *Will I be a better person?*

◆ *Does this goal mature me in Christ?*

◆ *Does this goal benefit others?*

◆ *Will others enjoy the rewards, too?*

If you can respond with a yes to these questions, you are headed in the right direction. A negative answer could signal a needed scriptural adjustment. Nothing is as refreshing as the satisfaction of knowing you are working for a God-given purpose.

You need to understand that walking by faith and striving toward Christ-centered goals is a process that may involve some occasional disappointments. But that does not mean that you are a failure or that somehow God has let you down. God's love has nothing to do with your performance.

Romans 8:35-39 says: "Who shall separate us from the love of Christ? Shall tribulation, or distress, or persecution, or famine, or nakedness, or peril, or sword? . . . But in all these things we overwhelmingly conquer through Him who loved us.

"For I am convinced that neither death, nor life, nor angels, nor principalities, nor things present, nor things to come, nor powers, nor height, nor depth, nor any other created thing, shall be able to separate us from the love of God, which is in Christ Jesus our Lord."

You cannot lose. Reaching out to strive toward a goal is always a good experience. When disappointment comes, you can treat it as a learning experience and keep on moving in wholehearted faith.

Genesis 24 tells a wonderful story of how faith and goals operate together. Abraham told his servant Eliezer to go into the land of his family to find a wife for Isaac, Abraham's son. The servant knew exactly what he needed to do, but he also knew that he could not get positive results through his own strength.

Before he went any farther, Eliezer prayed for God to grant him success. He then established an action plan in agreement with God's principles, trusting Him for completion. It wasn't very long before he arrived back home with Rebekah by his side. The real satisfaction of his adventure, and of yours as well, lies in seeing the Lord at work in your life. You are not alone in any endeavor. God promises to turn you in the direction you need to go at precisely the right time (Proverbs 16:9).

Do you desire to experience this type of satisfaction and joy? You can. You have everything to be excited about, especially in your relationship with a living and risen Savior who is bringing you into conformity to Him, working His will in your life until the day He brings you home to live with Him forever.

Isaiah 43:18-19 says: "Do not call to mind the former things, or ponder things of the past. Behold, I [God] will do something new, now it will spring forth; will you not be aware of it? I will even make a roadway in the wilderness, rivers in the desert."

Don't allow another day to pass without seeking God's plan for tomorrow and trusting Him to guide your feet along the path. You *are* somebody, because you have life through Christ and faith in a God who is perfect and holy and all-knowing. It is never too late to experience the awesome power of a God who loves you and desires to have one-on-one fellowship with you.

THE
HEART OF
PRAISE

"It is good to give thanks to the Lord,
and to sing praises to Thy name, O Most High;
to declare Thy loving-kindness in the morning,
and Thy faithfulness by night."
Psalm 92 :1

T he young man sitting across from me had good news. We had prayed for God's solution and direction with a certain issue for months. However, instead of celebrating God's goodness, he was on the brink of discouragement.

After prodding for the reason, he began to open up. "For weeks I prayed for God to turn my situation around. When the answer came, I was caught up in the idea of telling others what God had done. To be honest, I forgot to say thank You to Him. I don't even know if I know how to say thank you. Do I just say, 'thanks, God,' or what?"

My friend was a young Christian at the time, and what I eventually discovered through our times of counsel and prayer is that he had a sincere heart when it came to the things of God. He just needed the opportunity to learn how to praise God for His goodness and blessing.

Praise is an essential element to the Christian faith. Without it our spiritual lives are lifeless and mediocre. Very few of us come into the family of God knowing all there is to know about praise or, for that matter, any spiritual issue. We must learn and grow in our walk with Christ if we are to enjoy the Christian life.

God plants a desire within each Christian to learn and grow in this area, but it is up to us to praise Him for His wondrous love and goodness. What this young man was sensing was God drawing him close through praise and thanksgiving.

In *Thirty-One Days of Praise* author Ruth Myers writes: "It's not that praise is a sort of magical incantation that makes us strong in faith and maneuvers God into doing what we want. Rather, through praise we focus on God. We fix our inner eyes on Him with a basic trust in Him. Our praise springs from the simple response of faith, this simple choice to believe God; and praise in turn increases our confidence in Him."

One of the first things we learn concerning praise is to be sensitive to God's leading. Praise doesn't automatically come just to satisfy our need for spiritual feeling. It comes as an overflow of our awareness of God and His presence. You may find yourself suddenly aware of God's sensitivity to your needs. You may even be in prayer asking Him to provide wisdom for a specfic matter when you are hit with the reality that God does answer the prayers of those who love Him and have accepted His Son as their Savior. Praise comes for His splendor and mercy — for loving us in spite of our sinful nature.

Trials Can Be Avenues of Praise

Throughout history God had patiently taught and guided His people in the ways of praise. Many times their praise, like ours, came as a result of God's deliverance from some trial or tribulation. The Book of Ezra recounts the restoration of the Jewish people to their homeland following Babylonian Captivity.

Once they returned to Jerusalem, they found very little left of the temple. This was their only true place of worship, and it lay in ruins. Scholars tell us they began to sacrifice again amid the rubble. Yet it was not until they cleared away the fallen stones and laid the foundation for the rebuilding of the temple itself that they began to praise God once again.

"Now when the builders had laid the foundation of the temple of the Lord, the priests stood in their apparel with trumpets, and the Levites, the sons of Asaph, with cymbals, to praise the Lord according to the directions of King David of Israel. And they sang, praising and giving thanks to the Lord, saying, 'For He is good, for His loving kindness is upon

Israel forever.' And all the people shouted with a great shout when they praised the Lord because the foundation of the house of the Lord was laid." (Ezra 3:10-11)

Israel had spent nearly seventy years in Babylonian Captivity. Yet instead of bitterness over their fate, Ezra records their deep desire to reestablish a place of worship and praise to God. However their efforts did not go unchallenged. Israel's enemies rose up to discourage and defeat them. In Ezra and Nehemiah the people working on the temple and the rebuilding of the walls faced strong opposition.

Many times God uses our stiffest trials to teach us to trust Him and praise Him, even though our circumstances do not lend themselves to praise. True praise rises above the deepest valley to a place where sorrow cannot intrude. It is in God's presence that we find peace and victory over the enemy of our soul.

Praise is the overflow of joy and appreciation to God for who He is and what He has done. It is not to be limited to seasons of blessings but is appropriate in difficult times, hardships, trials, and times of persecution.

We cannot fully understand the power of praise until we have gone through times of despair and disappointment. When we begin to practice the principles of praise in times of heartache or stress, God transforms our circumstances — not always by bringing an end to our struggle, but by changing our perspective.

When our focus is on Him, we quickly learn that our faith is secure. We can trust Him no matter what befalls us because His Word tells us that He is faithful even when we are not (2 Timothy 2:13). It reminds us that God never leaves us.

Usually, Satan tries to deceive us into believing that God is not concerned about us because He would have never allowed trouble to come our way. The enemy wants you to doubt God and His ability to keep you and provide for you. But Psalm 91:1 states: "He who dwells in the shelter of the Most High will abide in the shadow of the Almighty." When you dwell with God, He never loses sight of you.

Israel had been with God in the hard times. Faithfully, He delivered them even though they had sinned greatly against Him. As the foundation to the new temple was being laid, Erza records how the people praised the Lord for His mighty and everlasting love. So intense was the moment and so mindful of where they had come from that the Bible says "Many of the priests and Levites and heads of fathers' households, the old men who had seen the first temple, wept with a loud voice when the foundation of this house was laid before their eyes." (Erza 3:12)

Tears can be reflections of praise to God. No where is it written that we have to smile or sing joyfully every time we praise our Savior. There may be times when tears are the only adequate expression of our heartfelt love and devotion to God.

God's Purpose for Praise

Helen Roseveare, a missionary doctor in the revolutionary-torn Congo region (now Zaire), was awakened one night by loud knocks on her bungalow door. She opened it to find soldiers seeking to ravage her house and physically assault her. During the mindless attack, all she could think was *Why had God allow this to happen?* His answer to her was: "Helen, they're not fighting you: these blows, all this wickedness, is against Me. All I ask of you is the loan of your body. Will you share with Me one hour in My sufferings for these who need My love through you?"

After the attack, she went home to England where she could heal emotionally and physically. During her time there, she wondered if she would ever be able to return to the Congo. Questions filled her mind as she wondered why God allowed this to happen.

It took time but God began to change her perspective on the situation. In her prayer time He gave her the word *privilege*. She began to see her trial as a *privilege* instead of a heartache. "He didn't take away pain or cruelty or humiliation," she says. "No, it was all there, but now it was altogether different. It was with Him, for Him, in Him. He was actually offering me the inestimable privilege of sharing in some little way in the fellowship of His sufferings."

In returning to the Congo, Helen Roseveare made the pilgrimage from trial and tragedy to victory and peace. "It was an unbelievable experience. [God] was so utterly there, so totally understanding. His comfort was so complete — and suddenly I knew, I really knew that His love was unutterably sufficient."

The King David writes: "O God, You are my God, earnestly I seek You; my soul thirsts for You, my body longs for You, in a dry and weary land where there is no water. I have seen You in the sanctuary and beheld Your power and Your glory. Because Your love is better than life, my lips will glorify You. I will praise You as long as I live, and in Your name I will lift up my hands." (Psalm 63:1-5, NIV)

Miles away from home and those he loved, David, the anointed king of Israel, ran for his life. For years he lived the forsaken life of a criminal. His friends were men whose reputations were dark. He was on the run from a

king who had gone mad with envy and rage.
One false move, one slip-up and Saul would
kill him.

How could David wake up in the morning
with praise in his heart? As a boy he taught
himself to play the lyre and sang songs of worship and praise to God. Little did he know
that when he grew older, he would sing those
same songs, which comprise much to the
Book of Psalms, out of a desperate need to
know God's closeness as a cover for protection and hope.

Praise changes the way we view our lives.
Had David focused only on his circumstances,
he would have become hopelessly discouraged. But he didn't allow himself to remain
fixed on the elements of his present situation.
He focused on God — on His love and
promises. He sang to the Lord "a new song"
and received the encouragement his heart
needed in order to continue doing what God
wanted him to do at that moment.

"In Thee, O Lord, I have taken refuge; let
me never be ashamed. . . . Blessed be the
Lord, for He has made marvelous His loving-
kindness to me in a besieged city. As for me, I
said in my alarm, 'I am cut off from before
Thine eyes;' nevertheless Thou didst hear the
voice of my supplications when I cried to
Thee. O love the Lord, all you His godly
ones!" (Psalm 31:1, 21-23)

ty Acts of God

ote concerning a
to give in to
see the salvation of
4:13) These words con-
and to the believer when he
great straits and brought into
ary difficulties. He cannot retreat;
nnot go forward; he is shut in on the
ght hand and on the left. What is he now to
do?

"The Master's word to him is 'stand still.' It will be well for him if, at such times, he listens only to his Master's word, for other and evil advisers come with their suggestions. Despair whispers, 'Lie down and die; give it all up.' But God would have us put on a cheerful courage, and even in our worst times, rejoice on His love and faithfulness."

God doesn't always change our circum-stances, but He will change our hearts and mold them into instruments of praise if we allow Him. The Apostle Paul prayed three times for God to remove a certain thorn of the flesh that buffeted him. Each time God reminded Paul that "*[His] grace is sufficient . . . for power is perfected in weakness.*" (2 Corinthians 12:9)

A vital part of praise is recalling the mighty acts of God. In 2 Chronicles 20:1-30 Israel

learned that it would soon come und
attack of some of their fiercest enemies
Jehoshaphat immediately went to God i
prayer. He found three things that were b
ficial to Israel's situation.

They were not to focus on their situation
but on God instead. This is what Helen
Roseveare did as well as King David. Instead
of becoming bitter and unforgiving, they
became receptive to God's will even though it
was hard to understand from a human standpoint. Jehoshaphat recognized the sovereignty
of God through praise (v. 6). "O Lord, the
God of our fathers, art Thou not God in the
heavens? And art Thou not ruler over all the
kingdoms of the nations?"

As we praise God for who He is — all powerful, all knowing, ever present — we are
made aware of His awesome care for us.
Affirming His sovereignty in every situation
fosters security and hope. God is ever for us.
He is never against us. How can we fail when
the sovereign ruler of the universe is on our
side? As Israel praised God in this way, the
Lord began to move in their behalf.

Jehoshaphat also recalled the mighty acts of
God. Likewise, the God who has delivered us
in the past will sustain us today. God had
brought the people out of Egyptian bondage,
divided the Red Sea, and provided food for
them in the wilderness. If He could do this,

He could surely save them from the approaching enemy forces.

On the day of the battle, instead of putting the fighting men up front, God instructed Jehoshaphat to position the choir in the lead. When the people marched into battle, they did so with the singers singing praises to God. The Bible says, "When they began singing and praising, the Lord set ambushes against the sons of Ammon, Moab, and Mount Seir, who had come against Judah; so they were routed." (v. 22)

Praise Is Rooted in Dependence on God

Praise paves the way for our dependence on God. When we begin to praise the Lord, we become aware of our need for God. As we praise Him, we extol His virtues, His omnipotence, and His mighty acts. We recognize our failures and weaknesses and see the need to cling to God.

Israel knew they were in a desperate situation, but they refused to become involved in self-pity. They moved on to stand in faith and trust God for His sovereign care.

When you feel as though the enemy is attacking you emotionally or mentally, make it a goal never to give him a moment of your time. If you hesitate and allow yourself to become engulfed in thoughts of self-pity, then more than likely you will suffer emotional defeat.

Faith is something you cannot reach out and touch. It is not a material force. It is spiritual, just as praise is spiritually linked to God in a very intimate fashion. If you wait until you can figure out what you need to do, then you will never grow in your spiritual life. Praise enlarges your vision and calls you to trust God, even though you don't understand how He will intervene. As you trust Him, you learn how He operates and how to respond to His leading.

When we praise God, rather than being drawn aside by thoughts of depression and darkness and doubt, we activate a faith-factor within us that cannot be shaken or distorted. We are the only ones who can yield to the enemy's attacks. God never yields; and as long as He is our goal, our hope, and the focus of our praise, we will come out the winners.

This is not to say that every single battle you face in life is going to end up just wonderful. God allows each of us to taste difficulty. Ruth Myers writes: "In 1960 my first husband, Dean Denler, was hospitalized in Hong Kong with terminal cancer. At that point praise took on a new importance in Dean's life. He decided that, through praise, he would make his hospital room a special dwelling place for God.

"'I'll be praising God for all eternity,' he told me, 'but only during my brief time on earth can I bring Him joy through praising Him in the midst of pain.'

"Some months later a close friend was officiating at Dean's funeral. He told those who had gathered, 'Dean's room became a sanctuary, his bed a pulpit, and all who came to comfort him were blessed.' Praise did not bring healing of Dean's cancer. But through praise and faith Dean brought the refreshment of God's presence into a painful situation, honoring God in death as he had in life."

If we never suffered or never felt the intensity of stressful pressure, then how would we know that we truly needed God. However, we can claim Romans 8:28: "God causes all things to work together for good to those who love [Him]." David learned to love the Lord when he was quite young. But the reality of God's awesome power and endless love did not fully register in his heart until he was put into tight places.

He learned that God did not abandon those He loved. He cried out to the Lord and saw how God protected him and fulfilled every promise that He had ever made. God does not have favorites, but He does have intimates.

God doesn't love one person more than

another. Those who love Him, praise Him, set the focus of their hearts on Him are known by God in an intimate way. God is willing to reveal Himself to anyone who values intimacy with Him as being something to be obtained.

In *Reflections on the Psalms* C.S. Lewis wrote: "Therefore praise not merely expresses but completes the enjoyment; it is its appointed consummation. . . . In commanding us to glorify Him, God is inviting us to enjoy Him."

Shout joyfully to the Lord, all the earth.
Serve the Lord with gladness;
Come before Him with joyful singing.
Know that the Lord Himself is God;
It is He who has made us, and not we ourselves;
We are His people and the sheep of His pasture.

Enter His gates with thanksgiving,
And His courts with praise.
Give thanks to Him; bless His name.
For the Lord is good;
His loving-kindness is everlasting,
And His faithfulness to all generations.

Psalm 100

When we worship God through praise we come away with an enlarged vision of who He is. Praise calms the heart because its focus is not on our present situation but Christ who is over all things. When our desire is to love God and serve Him, praise will flow out of us like a fountain. It's not limited to time, space, or style. It can be public or private. However, the goal of praise should never be to be seen or noticed but to worship God for who He is.

Requirements for Praise

The first requirement for praise is knowing the truth. Jesus Christ died for you. No matter what you did in the past, His love is available to you. His care for you is unconditional. In *The Power of Commitment* Jerry White writes: "God unconditionally commits. [He] is the Great Initiator of the eternal commitment — with Moses, with Abraham, with David, and finally with Christ in the New Covenant. When you commit yourself to someone, you care what happens to that person."

God cares what happens to you. He wants you to know Him on an intimate basis, but this takes commitment on your part. Do you love God enough to tell Him that you want to know Him and live for Him each day?

Salvation is the first step to living a life of praise. If you have never accepted Jesus Christ as your Savior, you can do this right now. Tell Him you love Him and realize you have not lived your life His way. Ask Him to forgive you and receive and live His life. Ask Him to teach you His ways and help you understand how to live the Christian life in freedom and truth.

Realize, the moment you pray for Christ to come into your heart He does just that. He transfers your life from one of eternal death to eternal life. There's nothing you can say or do to save yourself. Apart from accepting Christ as your Savior there is no eternal life. Also take time to ask God to forgive you of any known sin.

Perhaps you are living far from His will, and you wonder if He could somehow detour His love. God created you. No matter where you are He gave you life, and He loves you. He does not love sin, but He certainly loves you.

Sin, addictions, and situations often seem hopeless to us, but not to God. He will direct you in His Word, the Bible, to help you understand how you can leave temptation behind. Sometimes this requires talking with a Christian counselor or pastor. However, one thing is certain — God will not abandon you. If you ask Him to help, He will do it. He cleanses you from sin and frees you to walk in newness of life. (Romans 6:4)

The second requirement for praise is desire. We may not always know how to praise God;

but if we have a thankful heart, praise will flow out from it. One of the most powerful messages of God's love for mankind is found at the foot of the cross. Jesus was and is the Son of God. He could have chosen not to come to earth, but He did and He died for our sins so we might have eternal life.

His coming also meant that we could know the Father firsthand. Christ told His disciples, "He who has seen Me has seen the Father." (John 14:9) Pastor and author Jack Hayford writes, "With our appointment to worship, let's consider worship as a time we 'meet God.' We need to regularly come into the presence of God in worship, to encounter through worship. We have . . . 'an unalterable need of an altar.'

". . . Both public and private times of worship are needed in a disciple's life with Christ. Along with our gathering times with the church, let's also have times that we meet the Lord at private altars of worship, encounter, and growth."

God loves intimacy. He longs for us to share all of our hopes and dreams and fears with Him. Over time as we learn about who He is, a curious things begins to happen. We find ourselves asking Him more and more what He wants for our lives and thinking less and less about what we want.

Suddenly, praise becomes a natural part of our existence. The desire to sit at His feet and hear His voice grows intently as it did with Mary of Bethany. Praise fills our hearts because the Son of God calls us by name. We don't have to be afraid because our lives are hidden with Him. We live in this world but our true citizenship is in heaven with Him. You are His child, a joint heir with Christ.

Through praise our lives become Christ-centered. This means we are constantly on the lookout for how we can please God. Knowing that when we do, He blesses us in many ways. Blessing is always a result of obedience. And praise takes us to a point where we long to obey God.

We begin to discover His will and purpose for our lives. This is the natural outfitting of spiritual intimacy with Christ. His will and guidance is no longer a mystery but is revealed to us as we learn to trust and walk in close communion with Him.

The number one question people ask me is how can I know the will of God for my life or some specific situation? The answer is easy: Get alone with the Lord, and begin to praise Him for His love and care for you. Read His Word and ask Him to open your mind and heart to the principles written within its pages. As you do this, you will find that God's will becomes evident to you.

Prayer, praise, and meditation on God's Word will lead you to His will. There is no way to miss it if you are committed to doing what you know He wants you to do.

Begin your journey of praise by making a list of things that bring thoughts of thanksgiving. It could be something as simple as the sunshine or a friendship. You may be struggling with depression and feel as though there is very little to be thankful for. God knows your circumstances. When you hurt, He hurts. The road to recovery may seem long right now, but He will be with you every step of the way.

Worship God for His Ability to Understand

No matter how dark or black life appears, if you will let Him, He will bring flashes of light and hope to your world. He is our only true Source of encouragement. People fail us, but God never will. He has made a commitment to love, protect, and provide for you. You can be honest with Him. If praise is difficult you can tell Him all about it. Praise defuses depression. Over time and with God's help, you can chase away the dark moments by injecting praise into your life.

Be sure to address any known rebellion in your life. This can be a leading cause of discouragement. God wants you to do one thing, but you insist on doing something else. Therefore you find yourself in Jonah's shoes, on the run from God and struggling with a rebellious heart.

Admit what you are feeling. Tell God that you are having a difficult time seeing it His way, but you are open to understanding His truth. Crack open the door of your heart and allow Him to show you His plan and His desires for your life. God loves you, and He is not requiring perfection, only a willingness on your behalf to trust Him and allow Him to love you.

Praise accomplishes more than anything else can. It motivated God to save the nation of Israel from enemy attack, to establish David as king, and to send Christ to earth as our Savior and Lord. He is worthy of all our praise. And through Him we are given the hope and peace of eternal life.

I will bless the Lord at all times;
His praise shall continually be in my mouth.
My soul shall make its boast in the Lord;
The humble shall hear it and rejoice.
O magnify the Lord with me,
And let us exalt His name together.

Psalm 34:1-3

Spiritual Warfare

During the Gulf War, the eyes of the world were focused on the Middle East and the strife building in that region. In wartime there is always a threat of loss of life, dismissal of liberty, and emotional destruction. Rarely does a nation emerge from war without some kind of physical or psychological scars.

However, there is a war far more destructive than the ones fought on a battlefield. It is a spiritual war and it involves each of us. None of us is immune. The tragedy in this case is the fact that many do not realize they are in a battle. They ignore the warning signs and fail to recognize the enemy's destructive intent.

First Peter 5:8-10 tells us to: "Be of sober spirit, be on the alert. Your adversary, the devil, prowls about like a roaring lion, seeking someone to devour. But resist him, firm in your faith, knowing that the same experiences of suffering are being accomplished by your brethren who are in the world. And after you have suffered for a little, the God of all grace, who called you to His eternal glory in Christ, will Himself perfect, confirm, strengthen and establish you."

Identifying the Enemy

Scripture tells us that our enemy is not just one person in the form of Satan but an entire confederacy of evil spirits. "And having summoned His twelve disciples, He gave them authority over unclean spirits, to cast them out." (Matthew 10:1) The other thing that is very clear in Scripture is that the enemy and his forces are relentless in their pursuit of the body of Christ. Their goal is to keep men and women from coming to know Jesus Christ as Savior and Lord. This is why Peter wrote to the early church admonishing them to stand guard over their lives. He knew the enemy would stop at nothing to undermine God's plan in the life of a believer.

Author and Bible teacher Kay Arthur explains: "Clearly, Satan is not interested in the things of God. You can be sure he'll do everything he can to hinder you in your search for truth and understanding. Remember, he hates truth and will only use it when it's to his advantage, weaving it in with his lies to seduce you and lead you astray. And if that doesn't work, he'll seek to deceive you with signs and false wonders" (*Lord, Is It Warfare? Teach Me To Stand,* Multnomah Press).

While Satan's power is limited — he is not omnipresent, omnipotent, nor omniscient — he was created by God and has tremendous power, knowledge, and beauty. He does not tempt us with things that are repulsive or ugly but with things that appeal greatly to our senses. When we dismiss God's warning to beware of his evil against us, we set ourselves up for heartache and disappointment.

Satan will never tell you, "I'm your greatest threat." He comes as an angel of light — a counterfeit of God's truth. He has four objectives: to tempt you to doubt the Word of God; to distract you from spiritual things by overloading your schedule; to disable you in the Lord's service by running your witness through sin and guilt; and to destroy your usefulness physically and/or emotionally.

Many believers go to church, give their tithe, and yet are completely deceived by Satan's tactics. In the Gulf War, the one thing the commanders did not do was get in the foxhole with the enemy. They studied his movements so they could defeat him, but they never joined in on his activities. Far too many Christians open themselves up for attack by the enemy by frequenting places and doing things God never intended them to do.

God has called each of us to live a life of purity and holiness (Romans 12:1). Neither of these lead to boredom or isolation. Jesus' life was far from boring, and He certainly was not a loner. The Gospels are filled with accounts of Him reaching out to people, touching them, talking with them, eating with them, and listening to them tell of their deepest needs. God's love was all the motivation Jesus needed to sacrifice all He had so that you could enjoy all that God gives.

Another danger Christians fall prey to is simplifying the reality of Satan's presence. In *Weather of the Heart,* Gigi Graham Tchividjian recalls how when she was a child, she would sing a silly song about the devil. One night at dinner, all of the Graham children joined in on the chorus and to their surprise met their father's rebuke. With a serious look on his face, Graham said, "I don't want you to sing that verse anymore."

"We were taken aback, since he was an old softie and tended to spoil us. We all looked at him.

"'Why, Daddy?'

"'Because,' he replied, 'the devil is a good devil.'

"All of us — including Mother — burst out laughing. Then we noticed he looked very serious and the laughter died away.

"'What I mean,' he explained, 'is that the devil does a very good job of being a devil, and I think it is wrong to take him lightly or mock him. He is real and powerful, and he is no joking matter.'"

Many of us remember a comedian a few years back who made his living by telling stories of how he did bad things "because the devil made him do it." Satan loves this type of attention. It reduces his image to nothing more than a funny irritation. However, in recent years Hollywood has become tremendously bold in its depiction of demonic forces. You may wonder what Satan would reap from this type of exposure — plenty. His goal in exposing himself in this way is the same as what Graham described, and that is to lull us into thinking that none of what we see on television or at the movies is possible. He wants to trick us into thinking he doesn't exist, but don't be fooled. His deception is a narrow passageway that ultimately leads to destruction.

Behold, I Give You Power

In Luke 10:19, Jesus tells His disciples: "Behold, I have given you authority to tread upon serpents and scorpions, and over all the power of the enemy, and nothing shall injure you." He is speaking to them about spiritual matters and avoiding being captivated by the mind-set of this world. There is a reason for this; for now, God has allowed Satan to position himself as prince of this age. While his final fate is eternal death, today he is a force that must be recognized and dealt with accordingly. One of the most important principles we must learn as believers is that God's Word and the victory of Christ's death on the cross have broken his power. We do not have to shrink back in fear but can stand victoriously as long as the source of our strength is resting in Jesus Christ. Go up against him in human strength alone, and you will go down in defeat. It is only through the power of the blood of Jesus Christ that we are given authority over Satan's evil.

Prayer and taking our rightful position in Christ is our strong foundation. The strength of God sustains us in times of sorrow and extreme stress and disappointment. When we attune our hearts and minds to the presence of the Holy Spirit living inside of us, we enter into a realm of peace that Satan cannot access.

Notice in Luke that Jesus did not send out the seventy disciples without the proper equipment. He was with them in Spirit. He is our Emmanuel — God with us. In His omnipresence, He traveled with the disciples as they journeyed throughout Judea. Jesus never abandons us. He is our constant Savior and Lord. This is why these disciples had power over the enemy. They did not go in their own stead. They went in the power of God, which was the power of Christ.

Not only did Jesus go with them in Spirit, He also provided detailed instructions about how to handle the situations they faced. When you ask God for wisdom, He provides it. His heart is bound to us in love for all of eternity. When you are in trouble, God will be there with you. When you fall to temptation, He will come to you, but you must cry out to Him and acknowledge your need of Him.

When the disciples returned from their mission, they were greeted by Jesus, who was overjoyed at their success. He said to them, "I was watching Satan fall from heaven like lightning." (Luke 10:18) The disciples made a unique discovery when they focused their hearts on God and not on their circumstances, the enemy was defeated. A major reason we do not depend on God more is because we are prideful. We tell ourselves that we can handle life on our own — we don't need God. Or we refuse to surrender our lives to His purpose and control. We seek our own desires, without thought to God's will. Many times we end up feeling lonely and fighting thoughts of bitterness and fear all because we choose to do it our way. What we find is that self-centeredness is a deadly tool in the hands of the enemy.

Jesus made sure His disciples took nothing with them. Purses, bags, and shoes were left at home. Their dependence was solely on God and not on themselves. All He instructed them to do was to tell others of the coming of God's kingdom. They were not to get sidetracked on other issues. They were to stay focused on what the Lord had given them to do. So much of spiritual warfare has to do with focus. If you focus on pleasing the desire of your sinful nature, then sooner or later, you will yield to temptation.

Satan's primary target in the life of the believer is the mind. This is where sin begins — in our minds. The enemy places temptation at our feet, and we wonder what it would be like to touch it. The danger is that once we touch it, our sinful nature springs to life through our emotions. It is very hard to stop a runaway train that has no braking system. This is the way it is once our emotional feelers are pricked and we respond to their urging.

Through Adam's sin in the Garden of Eden, we have received a fallen nature. When we accept Christ as our Savior, we are given a new life and a new nature. However, because we live in a fallen world where sin abounds, we must now choose between sin and God's truth. We may know what is right, but because our old sin nature longs to taste the forbidden fruit, we find ourselves entangled in a fierce struggle. In Romans, the Apostle Paul tells us that the only One who can save us from this conflict is Jesus Christ. "Wretched man that I am! Who will set me free from the body of this death? Thanks be to God through Jesus Christ our Lord!" (7:24-25)

God has given you life so that you might bring glory to His name. In John 15:5, Jesus tells His followers: "Apart from Me you can do nothing." Every moment, every second of your life is spent in one of three ways — living in the will of God, satisfying your fleshy urges, or yielding to Satan's temptations. God's concern is that you would learn to discern between the three and choose the ultimate gift of life through submitting to His will and plan. He gave His life for you as an eternal payment for your sin. However, there is yet another reason Christ came to earth, and that was to extend God's holy power to each of us.

In Acts 1:8, Christ admonished His disciples to remain in Jerusalem until they received the power of God at the coming of the Holy Spirit. This power is the same type of power God used to raise Jesus from the dead. In Greek, the word for this type of power is *dunamis* — the same word we use for dynamite. It is a resurrection power that does not yield to Satan's bidding. When Christ empowers us, He gives us a miraculous portion of His power to be used for His glory. We can stand against the enemy because we have been given the power to do so by God.

Dr. R.A. Torrey points out: "In the Spirit's power it is our privilege to get daily, hourly, constant victory over the flesh and over sin. This victory is not in ourselves, not in any strength of our own. Left to ourselves, deserted of the Spirit of God, we would be as helpless as ever. It is still true that in us, that is in our flesh, dwelt no good thing (Romans

7:18). It is all in the power of the indwelling Spirit, but the Spirit's power may be in such fullness that one is not even conscious of the presence of the flesh.

"It seems as if it were dead and gone forever, but it is only kept in place of death by the Holy Spirit's power. If for one moment we were to take our eyes off Jesus Christ, if we were to neglect the daily study of the Word and prayer, down we would go. We must live in the Spirit and walk in the Spirit if we would have continuous victory (Galatians 5:16, 25). The life of the Spirit within us must be maintained by the study of the Word and prayer."

Dressing for the Battle

One of the first things we learn as a result of studying God's Word is that we have spiritual weapons of warfare at our disposal. In Ephesians, the Apostle Paul tells us to put on the entire armor of God, which is our daily protection against the enemy. Putting on the armor of God is not a one time act, but a continuous action that enables us to stand firm in our faith in Christ. "Put on the full armor of God, that you may be able to stand firm against the schemes of the devil. For our struggle is not against flesh and blood, but against the rulers, against the powers, against the world forces of this darkness, against the spiritual forces of wickedness in the heavenly places." (Ephesians 6:11-12)

Many wonder why there is an emphasis on being clothed in God's armor. One of the reasons is simple truth; the demons recognized Jesus and they will recognize you as one belonging to Him. Warren Wiersbe writes: "Demons have faith (James 2:19) but it is not saving faith. They believe that Jesus Christ is the Son of God with authority to command them. They believe in a future judgment (Matt. 8:29) and in the existence of a place of torment to which Jesus could send them ('the abyss,' Luke 8:31). They also believe in prayer, for the demons begged Jesus not to send them in the abyss. They asked to be sent into the pigs, and Jesus granted their request." In Luke 4:34, they were terrified at His presence and cried out to Him: "What do we have to do with You, Jesus of Nazareth? Have You come to destroy us? I know who You are — the Holy One of God!" Never argue with the enemy. If you discern he is trying to draw you into a debate, do what Jesus did. He commanded them to "Be quiet and come out of [the man who was possessed]!"

Christ never drew attention to Himself and neither should we. His entire life was devoted to glorifying the Father. The enemy loves to get us caught up in ourselves. This is a primary reason we should always use the name of Jesus when we pray against the enemy. Christ tells us to be humble, to be sober in spirit, and to allow God to exalt us at the proper time. "Humble yourselves, therefore, under the mighty hand of God, that He may exalt you at the proper time. . . . Be of sober spirit, be on the alert. Your adversary, the devil, prowls about like a roaring lion, seeking someone to devour. But resist him, firm in your faith." (1 Peter 5:6-9)

The armor, in and of itself, is not a magical defense against the enemy. Just repeating the verses written in Ephesians 6 will not save you from the enemy's attacks. It is in learning about the armor and our position in Christ that we understand the victory that is ours in even the deepest times of adversity. It is our faith in the truth or God that makes the armor so significant to spiritual warfare.

Sadly, I find very few Christians who take Paul's admonition seriously. They get up in the morning and hurry out the door because they are late to work or behind schedule in getting their children to school. When a football player goes on to the football field, he doesn't wear a coat and tie. He wears a football uniform complete with pads, helmet, and special athletic shoes. If we can understand the logic here, why is it so hard to understand that in order for us to be victorious in our walk with God, we must suit up spiritually? I usually begin each day by praying and asking God to clothe me in His armor. I also ask Him to prepare me for the situations I will face during my daily routine. You can do the same. The following is a short list detailing the armor and suggestions as to how to pray and ask God to fit you firmly with His protective care.

◆ Begin each morning by thanking God for His sovereign care over your life. Acknowledge the fact that the victory is yours no matter what you are facing, as long as you follow His battle plan. By faith, claim victory over _____ (I usually list any situation or decision I know I will face during the day.) Then claim each piece of the armor as your strong defense against the enemy.

◆ By faith put on the belt of truth. Thank God for His sovereign truth and for knowing you perfectly — all your strengths and weaknesses — and loving you completely. Acknowledge the fact that you are a new creature in Christ and have been set free from the power of sin. Satan never wants you to focus on your victory in Christ. Instead, he likes for you to begin each day feeling discouraged and defeated. His other tactic is to lure you into thinking you are smarter and more talented than others. God never blesses pride. Instead, His blessings are reserved for the humble and meek in spirit.

◆ Put on the breastplate of righteousness.

Ask God to guard your heart and emotions throughout the day. Pray that He also will keep you from being involved in anything that is impure or would cause you to yield to Satan's temptation. Realize that God never calls us to live by emotions; He calls us to live by faith based on His truth. The breastplate protects our will and emotions. Truth never wavers when confronted by adversity, but emotions always will.

◆ Claim the sandals of peace and surrender your life to the Lord for His purposes. Pray that you will learn to rest in the Lord during the day (Phil. 4:6-7). Incredibly, when you learn to do this you will find that His peace is adequate for every trial and heartache. But if you are hurting, never be afraid to tell Him. God will never make you feel guilty; He is your comfort, and He will protect your heart.

Also pray that you will be used by Him to touch others with His peace and hope by making you sensitive to the needs of those around you. There are so many people who are hurting and afraid to say anything for fear that they will be an imposition. Even if you can't give materially or financially, you can pray for the needs of others. Jesus was always giving Himself away. He was not afraid to reach out and touch the hurting nor was He repulsed by the sinner. He sought to eradicate sin while loving the sinner.

◆ Take up the shield of faith and stand firm in the love of God. Apart for the Lord, you can do nothing. But with Him you can do all things (Phil. 4:13). Nothing the enemy sends your way can penetrate God's loving shield of protection. He even tells us in Isaiah that He is our rear guard (52:12). We can go through the day without fear because the same God who set the entire universe in motion is the God who loves you and will provide for your every need. He shields you from Satan's evil intent. But there is a responsibility that you have as well. God can only do what you allow Him to do.

While He can and still does work miracles, if you refuse to follow His plan and knowingly do something outside His will, He allows you to go. He never forces you to do anything against your will. It is your choice how closely you follow Him. However, you need to know that sin has natural consequences. Satan has tripped up many believers by tempting them to go along a different path than what God has planned. For example, the shield of faith will do you no good if you insist in viewing pornography.

◆ Put on the helmet of salvation. As believers, the warfare we are engaged in is not physical; it is a battle fought within the mind, will, and emotions. Satan's habit is to bombard the mind with evil thoughts, fears, doubts, and jealousy. He knows if he can discourage us we will want to give up and, in doing so, will become useless for God. But the helmet of salvation protects our thoughts and offers a sure defense against tormenting thoughts. When you claim the helmet of salvation, you verbalize Christ's lordship over your life. You can choose to stop every impure and negative thought. I elect to take every thought captive to Christ and choose to dwell on all that is good and right and pleasing to Him (Phil. 4:8-9).

◆ Finally, take up the sword of the Spirit, which is the Word of God. Thank Him for the precious gift of His Word. For whatever situation you face, God has a purpose for allowing it and a plan for seeing you through it. By studying His Word, you build a power base in your mind. When trouble comes, the Holy Spirit brings the right Scripture to mind to help you victoriously combat the enemy. God's Word reminds us that we are under no obligation to satisfy fleshly desires (Romans 8:8-9). We are free from the power of sin because greater is He who is in you than he who is in the world (1 John 4:4). So by faith you can take up the strong sword of the Spirit, which is your sure defense.

The Victory Belongs to God

In *Reclaiming Surrendered Ground,* Christian counselor Jim Logan writes: "Your true belief is revealed by what you do under pressure. Most of us, during times of pressure, will not consider that a spiritual battle may be underway in our lives. But we are often in a fierce battle with the enemy of our souls. Spiritual warfare is a biblical reality. The question is not whether we wrestle demonic spirits, but who's on top? Do the spirits have us pinned? . . . The apostle Paul said he didn't want the Corinthian believers to be ignorant of Satan's devices (2 Corinthians 2:11), but the church of Jesus Christ today is woefully ignorant of the way our enemy works.

"Please understand that I am not talking about bizarre happenings or things flying through the air. . . . For the vast majority of Christians . . . spiritual warfare is another name for the daily battle we wage against 'all that is in the world, the lust of the flesh, and the lust of the eyes, and the pride of life' (1 John 2:16)."

Anytime we discuss spiritual warfare, it is important to remember that God has the final victory. At no point does He ask us to defend ourselves or to battle the enemy with our limited resources. Jesus told His disciples: "These things I have spoken to you, that in Me you may have peace. In the world you have tribulation, but take courage; I have overcome the world." (John 16:33) These are His words of hope to those who place their trust in Him. He has defeated the enemy and now reigns at the right hand of the Father, interceding on our behalf (1 John 2:1). Christ faced the temptations of Satan victoriously and provided a way for us to do the same.

One of Satan's favorite tools in the life of a believer is discouragement. He knows if he can discourage you and overwhelm you with feelings such as inferiority, guilt, and helplessness, you will be inclined to give up and lay aside your commitment for Jesus Christ. Make no mistake about it, he will go to any length to achieve his goal. In *The Adversary* Mark Bubeck writes: "The believer's emphasis in spiritual warfare must be upon a biblical, doctrinal approach to the subject. Subjective feelings, emotional desires, and fervent sincerity are not sufficient weaponry against Satan. He yields no ground to emotion or sincerity. He retreats only when faced with the authority of the Lord Jesus Christ and the truth of the Word of God."

The nonbeliever has much to sorrow over; they are spiritually blind and do not understand their ultimate end. A recent poll indicates that most people believe there is a hell, but that they will not end up there. When asked who would, many responded with names of fallen dictators and mass murderers. However, the truth remains unless they come to a point of realization and turn to God's Son for forgiveness, they will be ones to spend eternity separated from God in hell.

Jim Logan writes: "When it comes to God's people, evil spirits are spirits of influence only. That's not true for unbelievers in the world. They are held firmly in Satan's grasp, under his control, blinded in their hearts and minds and utterly dead to spiritual truth until quickened by the Holy Spirit. They are members of his kingdom of darkness (Ephesians 2:2)."

Far too many believers ride the fence spiritually and wonder why they suffer. They want to live for Christ, but yielding their lives completely to Christ seems too great a requirement. So with one foot in the world and the other in the kingdom of God, they wonder why true peace and contentment allude them.

When the commanders in the Gulf War sat down to talk strategy, their first objective was to know their enemy. As a Christian you need to know that Satan never gives up in his pursuit of you. He wants you to fall to temptation. And when you do, he is the first one to announce your failure.

God will never accuse you. He knows you perfectly and only desires to do what is best for you (Romans 8:1). His greatest goal is that you would come to know Him in a personal relationship. Because He is relational, He longs for our fellowship. Nothing can replace the friendship of God. Many times we think that people and things can bring us happiness. However, we quickly learn that no matter how much money we have or how many friends we acquire, without God we are lonely and needy.

Satan presents a pretty picture. He tells us that we have plenty of time to get to know Christ. He encourages us to run after things like popularity, fame, and fortune. He distorts the truth, entices us with immorality, and never mentions the consequences of our sin — the broken hearts, the tears, the low self-esteem that sin renders. He leads us down a darkened road, never telling us what it will cost us emotionally, physically, and mentally.

But you don't have to be deceived. Jesus Christ is your strong tower. And He will save you and give you hope. You can never be too much in love with the Lord Jesus Christ. And the closer you become to Him, the more you experience His peace in ways the world will never know. What is your best defense against the enemy — your love and devotion to Jesus Christ. As long as you remain in close fellowship with Him, you will be given the power and all the understanding needed to stand victoriously against Satan and his devices.

PART III

I Have Overcome
the World

FREEDOM THROUGH FORGIVENESS

Let us go to Calvary to learn how we may be forgiven. And then let us linger there to learn how to forgive.

Charles Spurgeon

E ach of us has experienced seasons of remorse, especially when we do something that violates the principles of God. These are the very moments we need to know that forgiveness is an essential part of fellowship with God. Those who fail to realize this can spend a lifetime bound by feelings of guilt and regret. Even though forgiveness has been bestowed in Christ, they struggle with a sense of inadequacy because of something that happened years ago. God's ultimate desire is that we would experience the freedom that comes from accepting His forgiveness and grace.

You may argue that your sin is too great for God's forgiveness, but this is not true. God is greater than any sin. His love for you is unconditional and eternal. The Bible tells us that when we seek His forgiveness, He will faithfully cleanse and forgive us. "If we confess our sins, He is faithful and righteous to forgive us our sins and to cleanse us from all unrighteousness." (1 John 1:9)

God has loved you from the beginning of time, appointing Jesus Christ to be your

Redeemer, Defender, and Intercessor.
(Isaiah 60:16; 25:4; Romans 8:34;
1 John 2:1) Today He is at the right hand of
God as your perpetual Advocate. His once
and for all sacrifice for sin secures your total
forgiveness. (Hebrews 10:14-18)

Jesus doesn't look at us and decide whether
we are good enough to merit His forgiveness.
He knows we're not. His forgiveness is
unconditional, based in His eternal love for
mankind and expressed in Christ's substitu-
tionary, sacrificial death on our behalf. If there
were something we could do (or not do) to
merit His forgiveness, then God's forgiveness
would not be based on grace. It would be
founded in performance.

Learning to Forgive Yourself

During my years in the ministry, I have met
countless people plagued by past sins. They
have never completely forgiven themselves.
However, the Bible tells us once we come to
God and confess our sins He is faithful to
restore us. He literally forgives and forgets. "I,
even I, am the one who wipes out your transgressions for My own sake; and I will not
remember your sins." (Isaiah 43:25) God
never brings up a past sin that has been confessed and forgiven. The believer is eternally
free from God's condemnation once he
embraces the Savior. (Romans 8:1) He no
longer lives in fear of punishment since Christ

bore his punishment on the cross.

Memories and feelings of guilt that haunt the believer are from our enemy and chief opponent, Satan, not from God. The best position to take when the accuser attacks is to acknowledge the position you have in Christ as a beloved child of God.

The issue of forgiveness was settled at the cross two thousand years ago. There's no need to plead or beg for God's forgiveness. The moment we confess our sin, God faithfully forgives it. However, many find this hard to accept, claiming it is too simple or that sin must be humanly atoned for. Jesus paid the atoning price at Calvary for our sin. If our enterprise could take away sin, we would not need a Savior. This is why God commands us to come to Him through His Son for the cleansing that is needed from sin.

In the book, *The Sensation of Being Someone,* Maurice Wagner writes: "[God] is sovereign in His authority over everyone. He is God. He is also honest. He does not hide the truth from us about ourselves. He starts with the fact that we are sinners. We have a reason for feeling as if we are nobody! We are guilty before Him, but He doesn't stop there. He has provided us a way of forgiveness and restoration. We cannot make ourselves acceptable; we must accept His grace to truly feel like somebody. When we do, we find that we always have been somebody to God, and His grace opens up a whole new premise for self-concept."

An important step toward true freedom is achieved the moment we learn to forgive ourselves. People spend years trying to bury and cover up emotional scars from the past. They may gain some satisfaction in forgiving others, but when it comes to forgiving themselves, the process turns ill-fated and dark. Forgiveness is the basis of the Christian life. For us to truly forgive others and move on in life, we have to see ourselves as forgiven and unconditionally loved by God.

If your life is haunted by past sin, then you know how difficult it is to enjoy life to the fullest. Much of the depression that besieges our society comes from laboring under an enormous load of guilt. Once we confess our sin to God, He forgives us and restores our fellowship with Him. To continue in unforgiveness is self-defeating. God has wiped away the sin; He remembers it no more. (Jeremiah 31:34) We are the ones who resurrect the memory of forgiven sin. Therefore, we are the ones who suffer.

One of the best ways I have found to put an end to old thoughts is to write out a confession to God, sign it, and date it. Then I go through the Scriptures concerning God's forgiveness. Write out each verse completely along with your confession. Once you have completed the project, read what you have written and what God has to say about you and any sin. Then across the page in BIG, BOLD letters write: "forgiven by God," because of His Son's love and death at Calvary.

Any time the enemy tries bringing up old news, take out the piece of paper and say, "Satan, I refuse to accept your lies. Jesus called you a liar and the Father of lies. Based on His death for my sins, I stand forgiven for eternity before God. I refuse and reject any attempt you may bring my way to get me to doubt what Christ has done for me. His death is sufficient payment for my transgressions, and I now stand accepted and loved by God."

Statements like these affirm our faith in God. When He sees our desire to trust Him, He rushes to our aid with encouragement and protection. Christian counselor and author, David Seamands writes in *Healing of Memories:* "This is yet another place where, standing under the cross of Christ, we need to make a definite decision to forgive ourselves and ask God to change our feelings toward ourselves. Just as [in Genesis] Joseph wept over his brothers' continued self-flagellation, God is grieved at our failure to forgive ourselves."

Forgiveness, in God's eyes, is the act of setting someone free from an obligation that resulted in a wrong done against another person.

Man's sin began in the Garden of Eden when Adam and Eve disobeyed God. Man was spiritually separated from God, and his sin passed down to each generation. But in His loving-kindness, God devised a way to set us free from the obligation of sin. Only when we accept Jesus Christ as our Savior is the power of sin broken and God's eternal forgiveness applied to our lives. Through Jesus Christ we have eternal forgiveness for *each and every* sin.

This doesn't mean you will never struggle with sin again. What it does mean is that sin no longer has the right to control you. "There is therefore now no condemnation for those who are in Christ Jesus. For the law of the Spirit of life in Christ Jesus has set you free from the law of sin and of death." (Romans 8:1-2) In the book *Living Free in Christ*, Neil Anderson writes: "When we have the life of Christ within us, we unwittingly bear the image of our heavenly Father more than we realize. The point is, Jesus saved us by bearing our sins upon Himself; therefore there is no condemnation, because we are forgiven."

One of God's attributes is love; therefore, He is motivated by love. (Jeremiah 31:3) Love is the reason Jesus died for your sins. Sin always requires a sacrifice. Christ's sacrificial death is sufficient payment for the sins of all of mankind. The way we receive God's eternal forgiveness is by acknowledging our sinfulness and asking Jesus Christ to come into our lives and cleanse us from all transgression. (Romans 6:23)

Free to Enjoy God

When we do this we are free to enjoy life to the fullest. We view life as much more than a long-running plateau. We find that it is made up of emotional and physical hills, valleys, and mountains. And while we learn that heartache, temptation, and suffering are part of the landscape, we also find we have a forgiving Savior to walk hand-in-hand with us over the varying terrain. On the way to discovering God's will, we anticipate times of overwhelming joy, laughter, and fellowship with others.

God isn't angry with you. He has placed within you the ability to withstand the hurtful blows of life. He is not "out to get you." God seeks to love and guide you, not to hurt or destroy you.

If sin is present, you can be sure God will convict you through the ministry of the Holy Spirit, but any discipline is a result of His abiding love. It is sent with the intention to steer you into obedience, not frustration. Realizing that God loves you and always seeks to restore your fellowship with Him is a key to the joyous Christian life.

If you have difficulty accepting His forgiveness, then you will have a hard time enjoying
His presence. You also will find it difficult
to forgive others. Bitterness and anger are
often the result of a distorted view of God's
forgiveness. The unforgiven become the
unforgiving. Talk to anyone who refuses to
forgive and you will find hurt, resentment,
and a lack of acceptance of God's forgiveness
in his or her own life.

There are consequences to sin. King David's
life bears witness to this. But his life is also a
testimony to the fact that God's love and forgiveness are unconditional. David wrote:
"How blessed is he whose transgression is forgiven, whose sin is covered! How blessed is
the man to whom the Lord does not impute
iniquity, and in whose spirit there is no
deceit!" (Psalm 32:1-2) He learned there was
only one place of true forgiveness, and that
was in the arms of God. Only in Christ can we
find genuine mercy and freedom from sin.
Man may be able to improve himself to some
degree, but he can never cleanse the stain of
sin from his life — only Jesus can do this.

John writes: "My dear children, I write this
to you so that you will not sin. But if anybody
does sin, we have one who speaks to the
Father in our defense — Jesus Christ, the
Righteous One. He is the atoning sacrifice for
our sins, and not only for ours but also for the

sins of the whole world." (1 John 2:1-2, NIV)

Jesus came into this world as a man to die upon the cross to bear the penalty of our sin. All of our sinfulness was placed on Him at Calvary's cross. God in His mercy accepts the atoning death of His Son as payment for our sins — past, present, and future. We are justified (proclaimed not guilty) in the eyes of God because Jesus died in our stead. Therefore, we are set free from sin's power. We are liberated to be all that God has planned for us to be. And we can now enjoy His fellowship through the presence of His Holy Spirit in our lives.

You don't have to worry about making the appropriate sacrifice — spending time in penance, performing certain tasks, observing specific rituals, behaving in a prescribed manner. Jesus is your sacrifice. God accepts and loves you just the way you are. The key to forgiveness is not what you do, but whom you know. It is only found in Jesus Christ the Son of God. He is the One who died for you that you might have eternal life. (John 3:16)

Forgiveness that flows from grace is the core of the gospel message, but God doesn't want us just praying "forgive my sins" and then continuing on in a unconcerned way. Salvation impacts every aspect of life. When we accept God's forgiveness for our sins, we gain a deeper understanding of God's nature, which should propel us into the delight of obedience. Forgiveness opens the door to an intimate, loving relationship with the Creator of the universe. Nothing is grander than this.

Handling Our Hurts

I knew a young man who had always wanted to be a doctor. He studied hard in school and graduated in the top percentile of his class. But when it came time to leave home, his father refused to let him go. He was forced to remain on the family farm and work. By the time he was twenty-three, he had all he could take and left home with a heart full of bitterness and resentment toward his father.

However, the anger didn't stop there. He did not get along with others. Whenever people tried to build a friendship with him, they immediately sensed his bitterness. He struggled with feelings of rejection and isolation. Finally, he met a young woman. They fell in love and married, but shortly after the wedding an unexpected outburst of anger marked the beginning of forty years of painful turmoil for his loyal wife. His vile language and violent temper eventually drove his wife's friends away. The poison of bitterness continued until his dying day — all because he was unwilling to deal with the rejection and hurt he had suffered as a teenager.

There is no way to know why this man's

father refused to let him leave home. Maybe the father was uneducated and felt threatened by his son wanting to go to college. Selfishness may have been the problem as the father didn't want to lose good help. The son may have been justified in his feelings. However, in the end, his actions only hurt himself. He was the one that bore the weight and consequences of his unforgiveness. The father died, but the son's bitterness remained. An unforgiving spirit is like a hot coal. The longer and tighter it is held, the deeper it burns. If not attended to, it can scar a person for life.

A spirit of unforgiveness doesn't develop overnight. It takes time for the hurt and anger to grow into the bitterness and resentment that characterize an unforgiving spirit.

In the years I have been a pastor, I have discovered there are distinct stages to dealing with and overcoming the circumstances that wound our spirit.

Feelings of hurt — We suffer an injustice, physical or verbal, and the impact is registered in our emotions. Often we are hurt in our young and formative years by those we love and respect the most. All hurt is really some form of rejection, though it may not be perceived as such at first. Most pain, isolation, fear, embarrassment, hatred, and other negative emotions all relate to rejection. We long to be accepted, but someone we love and trust rejects us. Feelings of rejection set the stage for developing an unforgiving spirit.

Confusion — This is a frequent response to hurt. We are bewildered that someone offends us and we struggle for an explanation, often flinching at the pain. In our perplexity, we sometimes question God's goodness and our faith fluctuates perilously.

Looking for a detour — When pain comes, the natural reaction is to find a way to block or remove the pain. We avoid anything that reminds us of the hurt, especially the person who inflicted the wound.

Digging a hole — After scheduling our lives in such a way as to avoid the pain, we try to forget what actually happened. Essentially, we dig a hole and try to bury the problem. Such isolation only intensifies the problem.

Denial — We tell ourselves and others it really doesn't hurt or that we have dealt with the problem and forgiven the person for the injustice. This can be a hard stage to overcome. Consequently, many people carry bitterness throughout life, demonstrated by a short fuse, negative behavior, and a refusal to see the connection between their anger and the offending incident.

Feelings of defeat — Regardless of how much we try to hide or bury the hurt, it usually finds a way of surfacing. Oversensitivity, shyness, a critical spirit, jealousy, envy, a short temper — all can be symptoms of an unforgiving spirit that results from rejection. A person can pray, change jobs or friends, make resolutions, and work hard to be different; but until he deals with the root of the problem, his behavior will be futile.

I have seen people deal with the anger and hurt they have carried for years and receive freedom. The recovery always came once the root of unforgiveness was uncovered, acknowledged, and dealt with.

Discouragement — This is usually the stage when people seek help or sink further into bitterness. God always seeks to encourage. He has a plan for your life. Don't let a lack of forgiveness keep you from experiencing His deepest love and steadfast peace. If you get help you will then be ready for the next stage.

Discovering the truth — Through the help of Scripture, a Christian counselor, pastor, or trusted friend, a person discovers the root of his unforgiveness. Not only is the truth found, but insight into feelings and inappropriate behavior is revealed. Finally, the pieces of the puzzle begin to fit together.

Taking responsibility — The person stops blaming others, owns up to his actions, and opens his heart to the healing power of God.

This is where memories are healed, though some are very painful. The person realizes that there is a hope waiting for him. God will not abandon him. Jesus understands what he feels because He also suffered rejection and abuse. Through the strength and compassion of Christ the person is able to come through this time of honest, open confession.

Deliverance — The conclusion is a beautiful, fresh sense of God's personal love. Any time we choose to forgive those who have hurt us, we are positioned to enjoy life at its best. Hostility is defused; grace is experienced.

God is positive-minded. He never thinks negatively. He is always moving toward the future, not the past. When He sees you He sees His Son in you and the tremendous potential within your life. When you forgive, you are free to move forward through Jesus Christ. You become the victor with Christ's help. When you refuse to forgive, your hurt controls your life. One of the saddest things I have encountered is a person saved by the grace of God but trapped in a web of unforgiveness. Break free now — choose forgiveness!

In *The Friendship Factor,* Alan Loy McGinnis writes: "The forgiving person is sometimes caricatured as weak and spineless, but the opposite is true. One must be strong to forgive, for forgiveness is a very positive force. It changes both you and your beloved. . . .

"You can't be free and happy if you harbor grudges, so put them away. Get rid of them. Collect postage stamps, or collect coins, if you wish, but don't collect grudges. Just as bitterness produces more bitterness in others, so love begets love."

Why We Refuse to Forgive

If you refuse to forgive those who have hurt you, you probably will experience one or more of the following problems.

Selfishness — What happened to you was unfair. But instead of turning to God, you turn to thoughts about yourself — how foolish you looked, how you did not get your way. Feelings of anger take root as you consider how your rights were violated. Soon bitterness sinks its tap root deep into your heart as you adopt an attitude that believes the world must come to you on its knees before you even think about forgiving.

Pride — This often is the primary reason a person fails to choose to forgive. Pride proclaims, "How dare she hurt me." "If I forgive him, it will appear that I am weak." "I must make him pay for what he has done." When pride is active, forgiveness is difficult.

Low self-esteem — People who struggle with feelings of low self-esteem often feel insignificant. They make the mistake of attaching their worth as a person to the wrong they have suffered. As Christians, our significance is in Christ. We are to look only to Him for our self-worth. Christ views each of us as His beloved child. He knows our flaws, and He continues to love and nurture us. However, when we base our identity on someone's reaction, we essentially tell God that we are more worried about the evil done to us than the victory He holds for us in heaven.

This is God's word of instruction to us. We are to keep our minds focused on Christ. "For those who are according to the flesh set their minds on the things of the flesh, but those who are according to the Spirit, the things of the Spirit. For the mind set on the flesh is death, but the mind set on the Spirit is life and peace." (Romans 8:5-6) To know true freedom, you need to forgive those who have wronged you and move on with your life.

You think you already have forgiven — Corrie Ten Boom writes in *Tramp for the Lord:* "Forgiveness is the key which unlocks the door of resentment and the handcuffs of hatred. It breaks the chains of bitterness and the shackles of selfishness. The forgiveness of Jesus not only takes away our sins, it makes them as if they had never been."

At one point in her life, Corrie thought she had forgiven a certain Christian couple for something they had done to her. Years passed and she maintained that she had extended forgiveness completely. One day, the subject of what this couple had done to her came up in a discussion with a friend. She quickly responded by saying: "I have long since forgiven them." Yet she walked over to her desk and produced a small stack of aging letters. They contained the evidence of the wrong done against her. Corrie had tried to forgive, but she had not forgotten.

Immediately, she went to God in prayer, "Lord Jesus, who takes all my sin away, forgive me for preserving all these years the evidence against others! Give me grace to burn all the blacks and whites as a sweet-smelling sacrifice to Your glory.

"I did not go to sleep that night until I had gone through my desk and pulled out those letters — curling now with age — and fed them all into my little coal-burning grate. As the flames leaped and glowed, so did my heart. 'Forgive us our trespasses,' Jesus taught us to pray, 'as we forgive those who trespass against us.' In the ashes of those letters I was seeing yet another facet of His mercy. What more He would teach me about forgiveness in the days ahead I didn't know, but tonight's was good news enough."

Forgiving someone seems too painful —
Forgiveness can be especially hard if the
wrongful hurt has been buried or hidden.
Incest, child abuse, rape, an extramarital affair,
severe beatings, or verbal abuse are hurts that
can damage even the strongest individual.
When dealing with deep hurts like these, it
may be wise to seek trusted Christian counsel-
ing through a pastor or qualified counselor.
Many times a trustworthy friend can help by
listening and offering support.

Forgiveness is something that comes from
within. God may not require you to go to that
person and work everything out but He does
want you to bring your pain to Him in prayer.
The reason He calls us to forgive is so that we
might enjoy His forgiveness. The way to freedom is paved with forgiveness and humility
before God.

The Scriptures emphatically exhort us to
forgive sin the same liberating way Christ has
forgiven us. "Bearing with one another, and
forgiving each other, whoever has a complaint
against any one; just as the Lord forgave you,
so also should you." (Colossians 3:13) Make a
list of those who have hurt you deeply. Then
ask God to help you forgive them for what
they have done. After you have prayed, write
"forgiven and freed" across their names.

Forgiveness — A Personal Matter

Forgiveness is something all of us will have to deal with at some point in life. We each face varying degrees of injustice. Some are easy to overlook; others take time. Regardless, the process of forgiveness cannot be ignored.

If you want to become what God has created you to be, forgiveness needs to be an integral part of your lifestyle. When you refuse to forgive, your relationship with God suffers. It is hard to worship and grow in your love for Him when there is unresolved hurt.

Regardless of the painfulness of your past, God wants to cleanse and restore your joy and hope. This is why forgiveness is so liberating. It frees us from the burden of guilt, bitterness, and anger and gives us a new purpose for living. Ask God *now* to make His forgiveness and unconditional love toward you very real. A life of praise and glory to God and His Son, the Lord Jesus Christ awaits you.

How to
Triumph
over
Temptation

The word *temptation* brings to mind something different for everyone. Some have a problem controlling their tongues, while others battle the urge to take drugs or consume too much alcohol. Many fight a private war with sexual addictions.

Whatever you may struggle with, understand that you are not alone; you are not the only one who has a tough time making the right choices. Temptation is defined as "the enticement to commit an unwise or immoral act, especially for a promised [or perceived] reward." That is what makes decision-making such a strain. The good option can look unappealing on the surface, while the negative one holds allure.

We feel tension when deciding between what we should do and what we shouldn't do. This struggle is not imaginary; the "should I or shouldn't I" questioning is not an isolated intellectual excercise. An actual war is going on inside us.

The root of this conflict is called *sin*. All of us are born sinful by nature and separated from God; that is, we have the innate desire to live life our own way instead of God's way.

The only solution for this separation from God is in His Son Jesus Christ, who died on the cross to pay the penalty for sin and reconcile us to God. (Romans 6:23; John 3:16)

So Why Does It Look So Good?

When you accept Christ's payment for sin and trust Him as your Savior, you have officially died to sin. What does this mean? *Dead* means that sin no longer has the power to force you to do or think anything. (Romans 6:1-3, 10-14) Of course, sin still exists as an influence, but its reign is broken. Sin has access to you, but no authority over you. You are free to choose against sin; its mastery has been broken. As a believer, you are free to say no.

In Christ, you have a new life and a new spirit. (2 Corinthians 5:17) The Holy Spirit, who indwells you the moment you place your trust in Jesus, enables you to choose obedience over rebellion. Even so, the pull from sin can be strong at times.

The Appeal Is Real

It is important to understand that your natural desires are God-given and legitimate. For example, there is nothing wrong with wanting to eat. But when you want to eat more or less than you should, or in a fashion that injures your body in some way, then the desire becomes illegitimate. Anytime you go beyond the loving boundaries God has set, you tread on sinful ground.

The first reaction when we yield to temptation is to blame someone else, blame the past, blame personality flaws. "My friend pushed me into it," you rationalize. Or "My parents raised me this way; I can't help myself." This tactic of shifting the guilt to another is not new. When God called to Adam in the Garden of Eden after he had sinned, Adam blamed Eve. (Genesis 3:12)

Why do we do this? It is tough admitting that the problem is our own. You probably have heard many times the excuse "the devil made me do it," and you may have used it yourself. Satan does, in many cases, play a role in temptation; but this statement simply is not true.

Satan can never *make* you do anything. His only powers are manipulation and deceit. (2 Corinthians 11:3; John 8:44) He can make you want to do or say something very badly, but he cannot literally force you to do it. Yes, Satan is a formidable foe, and his intent to entrap and snare never changes. Jesus gives this warning: ". . . He was a murderer from the beginning, and does not stand in the truth, because there is no truth in him. Whenever he speaks a lie, he speaks from his own nature; for he is a liar, and the father of lies" (John 8:44).

In 1 Thessalonians 3:5 and Matthew 4:3, Satan is referred to as the tempter, responsible for luring many to go astray. He continually seeks your weak and vulnerable spots and exploits them when given the opportunity. (1 Peter 5:8) Nevertheless, as Job 1:12 reassures, his abilities are limited by God.

God does not tempt you to sin, either. His character will not allow Him to. In no way can holy, almighty God be associated with sin. James 1:13-14 says: "Let no one say when he is tempted, 'I am being tempted by God'; for God cannot be tempted by evil, and He Himself does not tempt any one. But each one is tempted when he is carried away and enticed by his own lust."

No matter what the pressure, the inducements, the enticements — Scripture makes it clear that you are the one responsible for the sin, and no one else. When you are tempted, you may say yes or no. It is your decision, and despite the strong negative influence of temptation, you can make the right choice with God's help. Once you recognize the true nature of the conflict, you are prepared to put God's Word into action in every challenge.

The Way to Say No

What is your primary area of conflict? Right now, think about what causes you the most trouble, what makes you stumble the most often.

Write it down in the space below.

Most people have more than one, but focus on a single area for now. As you experience the joy that comes from seeing God's liberating truth in action, you can apply the principles of victory to other trouble spots.

Through every step in confronting temptation head-on, keep this in mind: Jesus knows what it feels like to be tempted. He identifies with you in every way and can personally help you in the time of crisis and decision.

Consider Jesus' confrontation with the devil in the wilderness. (Matthew 4) Jesus had not eaten in forty days; He was physically and emotionally exhausted, and that is precisely the time Satan chose to confront Him with his most potent attacks. With every offer the devil made, Jesus experienced the real tug of worldly desires. And even though this is the only account in Scripture of specific temptation directed by the devil against Christ, we can be sure that Jesus encountered it on many occasions just as we do.

Hebrews 4:15-16 says: "For we do not have a high priest who is unable to sympathize with our weaknesses, but we have one who has been tempted in every way, just as we are — yet was without sin. Let us then approach the throne of grace with confidence, so that we may receive mercy and find grace to help us in our time of need" (NIV). Hebrews 2:18 gives us this comfort: "For since He Himself was tempted in that which He has suffered, He is able to come to the aid of those who are tempted."

◆ *Know that in Christ the victory is yours.*

Patrick Morley writes this in *Walking with Christ in the Details of Life*: "Satan is less powerful than one 'temptee' who relies on the Holy Spirit to resist. For Satan to go up against one surrendered saint filled with the Holy Spirit is like a bantam-weight boxer standing before the explosive fury of a heavyweight champion-of-the-world's knockout punch. He's going to lose."

Whether you are confronted by Satan's craftiness, or pressured by desires within, or attracted by fleshly allures, Jesus has already made you the champion. (Romans 8:37) There is no such thing as a temptation too strong for you to resist, no matter what the circumstances or your emotional or physical state.

Understanding this truth from
1 Corinthians 10:13 is the key to conquering:
"No temptation has overtaken you but such
as is common to man; and God is faithful,
who will not allow you to be tempted beyond
what you are able, but with the temptation
will provide the way of escape also, that you
may be able to endure it."

Even when a situation seems to close in
around you, you have God's promise that
there is a way out. He will deliver you.
2 Peter 2:9a says: "The Lord knows how to
rescue the godly from temptation." Further,
He will not allow the pressure to be more
than you can bear in His strength. Remember
that in Christ, you do have the power to overcome, but you must apply it. Turn to Him
immediately and ask for His discernment to
find the escape hatch. He is faithful to deliver
you.

◆ *Be aware of your weakness and always stay
on the alert.*

In sports, teams build a good defense by
looking ahead to likely challenges and putting
together protective strategies. The same is
true of spiritual defense.

In his book *A Faith That Endures*,
J. Dwight Pentecost writes: "Just recognizing
the area(s) in which Satan regularly attacks
you is a giant step toward realizing victory.

Remember — Jesus had victory over the full force of Satan's temptations in every area, and He can provide victory for you, too. But we must go to Him first; waiting to turn to Him until after we've tried to solve the problem ourselves will almost always end in disaster."

Have you ever noticed that tempatation can hit the hardest when your guard is down? Jesus told His disciples just before He was betrayed: "Keep watching and praying, that you may not enter into temptation; the spirit is willing, but the flesh is weak." (Matthew 26:41) A consistent prayer life is a potent weapon for recognizing and resisting temptation.

◆ *Respond with the truth of Scripture.*

Be careful that you do not fall into error in the opposite direction by focusing excessively on your vulnerabilities. Overemphasizing your weakness, especially during the temptation itself, can be perilous.

When the pressure is on, avoid saying "I'm so weak," or "this gets me every time." Jesus has forgiven you, and He wants you to move forward in confident faith. (Philippians 3:13-14) Your cry for help should be God-centered, not self-centered, and should affirm His promises. State the positive truth of deliverance from 1 Corinthians 10:13. You may be weak, but Christ is your strong help.

When Jesus confronted Satan in the wilderness, He did not argue, justify, or debate. He quoted Scripture to counter each of the devil's false claims, and Satan was silenced immediately. No half-truth and no deceitful or cunning rationalization can stand in the face of God's Word.

It is a wise plan to have other verses prepared that deal with your most common trouble points. (See the Scripture reference guide at the end for suggested verses in key areas.) Memorize them for quick reference, or you may want to write them on small cards and carry them with you. The point is to be prepared. Take time now to write down a Scripture verse that pertains to the specific temptation you noted before.

_____

_____

_____

_____

_____

_____

◆ *Approach every opportunity, invitation, and relationship in light of your present state of mind and feelings.*

In other words, even though you have dealt with a particular temptation with success in the past, do not assume that you have that problem "under control" from now on. In each instance of temptation, the circumstances are slightly different. Yesterday you might have been emotionally steady or upbeat, but today you might be dealing with discouragement. Your emotional, physical, or spiritual condition can change the way you react to a given difficulty. Treat each time of testing as a separate case and turn to the Lord for the right perspective.

◆ *Stay away from the "how far can I go" mind-set.*

You place yourself in perilous territory when you ponder how close you can get to sin without actually sinning. When you stand right on the line, it takes only a small nudge to push you over. Position yourself correctly by thinking, "How can I become more Christlike in character through this testing?"

Maintain a commitment to spiritual growth and a heart for maturity. Like Paul, make it your goal to press on to know the Lord. "Not that I have already obtained it, or have already become perfect, but I press on in order that I

may lay hold of that for which also I was laid hold of by Christ Jesus. Brethren, I do not regard myself as having laid hold of it yet; but one thing I do: forgetting what lies behind and reaching forward to what lies ahead, I press on toward the goal for the prize of the upward call of God in Christ Jesus."
(Philippians 3:12-14)

◆ *Think about the future.*

Maybe you are wondering why it is so important to resist temptation. After all, in Christ your sins are forgiven, wiped away completely. That is true, but engaging in sinful behavior still carries consequences, some of which can be very damaging to others as well.

As you seek God's direction in your struggle, ask Him to give you wisdom to discern the results of sin. In a moment of crisis, it is sometimes easy to gloss over reality with justifications such as, "this isn't so bad," "it's not going to hurt anybody," or "I can quit whenever I want to."

Joseph, in the Old Testament, had plenty of opportunities to give in to the temptations of immediate gratification. (Genesis 37, 39–41) When his brothers sold him into slavery, he could have become angry and tried to hurt them in return. When he was falsely accused by Potiphar's wife and thrown in prison, Joseph could have become bitter and refused to acknowledge these events as part of God's plan. Finally, years later when his brothers came to Egypt seeking food, Joseph could have remembered their past wrongs and sent them away hungry. Yet through it all, Joseph resisted the urge to do the "natural, human thing" and take care of himself his own way. In each instance he saw past the appeal of the moment to the future God promised him.

◆ *Understand that God uses temptation to build His character into your life.*

Answer these questions while you are choosing a course of action. 1) If I give in, do I really understand the full consequence of my act of disobedience? 2) Am I willing to pay that price? 3) Is it true that ___ will satisfy me and bring true fulfillment according to God's plan?

If you respond with a "no" to any of these, put on the brakes! God is giving you His perspective on your situation and stripping away layers of self-deception and skewed reasoning.

Understand that God uses temptation to instill His character into your life. A temptation is really a strength-building test. (In the original Greek, the same word is used interchangeably for *temptation* and *test*.) Each time you are tested, you flex your spiritual muscles and develop them for success in future encounters. (James 1:2-4) Having God's viewpoint on temptation is a tremendous help: "In this you greatly rejoice, even though now for a little while, if necessary, you have been distressed by various trials, that the proof of your faith, being more precious than gold which is perishable, even though tested by fire, may be found to result in praise and glory and honor at the revelation of Jesus Christ." (1 Peter 1:6-7)

◆ *Build accountability.*

God did not design you to cope with every matter on your own. He wants you to have relationships with other believers for edification, instruction, fellowship. (Hebrews 10:23-25) Should you start to slip into error or need guidance, it's beneficial to have a mature Christian friend with whom you can share your problems. Your brothers and sisters in Christ act as a safety net for your aid and protection. If you would like to build such relationships, join a small group Bible study or service team where you can develop one-on-one contacts.

◆ *A special note —*

Some temptations and urges have deep roots that involve complex emotions or past experiences. If you have struggled with a problem for some time, or want further help in realizing Christ's lordship in a certain area, you may want to contact a professional Christian counselor.

What to Do When You Fail (Again)

One of the wonderful blessings of knowing Jesus as Savior is living in the goodness of His grace. When you mess up, when you blow it, when you do the very thing you never wanted to do again, He is there with arms open wide.

The apostle Paul expresses the situation this way: "For the good that I wish, I do not do; but I practice the very evil that I do not wish. . . . Wretched man that I am! Who will set me free from the body of this death? Thanks be to God through Jesus Christ our Lord!" (Romans 7:19, 24-25a)

The moment you first realize you have done wrong, turn to Him right away. Do not delay and allow unnecessary guilt and fear to build in your heart and hinder your fellowship with Him. He does not want you to bear a load that He has already taken on Himself. 1 John 1:9 says: "If we confess our sins, He is faithful and righteous to forgive us our sins and to cleanse us from all unrighteousness." God hates sin, but He loves you.

Remember, there is no limit to His grace; all of your sins — past, present, and future — are covered by His blood. The act of confessing is agreement with God that your sin is not pleasing to Him. Once you have confessed and repented (turned aside) from the sin, then you need to experience the reality of His finished work and forgive yourself. Replaying the "tapes" of past failures is negative, demotivating, and demoralizing. The apostle Peter denied His Savior and dear Friend three times, but he did not dwell on his failure and betrayal. Christ forgave him, and Peter moved on. (Luke 22:54-62; John 21:15-17)

You also need to understand that the consequence(s) of what you did might not go away. God may allow the natural result of sin to stay with you as a reminder and teaching tool, or He may remove the negative impact entirely. Avoid comparison with others and accept what He chooses with thanksgiving. (Hebrews 12:6-10)

No matter what happens, you can rest in the promise of Romans 8:28: "And we know that God causes all things to work together for good to those who love God, to those who are called according to His purpose."

Some Common Misconceptions

◆ *Fallacy – Being tempted is the same thing as actually sinning.*

Sometimes temptation packs an incredible punch to the emotions. One quick thought, and suddenly you feel the overpowering urge to yield. The longing begins, and you hear a voice saying, "Go ahead. Give in. You're already guilty. A good person would not think those things in the first place. You've already thought about it; what's the difference?"

The truth is there is all the difference in the world; temptation does not equal sin. Even the most cautious Christian hears and sees things that stir up ungodly thoughts and desires. You are not responsible for what others do or say or wear, and you cannot consistently control your environment.

What God does want you to do is immediately put every thought into submission to Him. ". . . We are taking every thought captive to the obedience of Christ." (2 Corinthians 10:5)

◆ *Fallacy – Spiritually mature Christians are not subject to temptation.*

This is absolutely not true, although the tendency is to believe that those who have walked with Christ for a longer time have advanced beyond certain temptations and daily struggles.

All of us will face temptation for the rest of our lives; that is a guarantee. In fact, as you grow in Christ, you will at times notice an increase in the intensity of temptation. The more you are conformed to the likeness of Jesus, the more you are able to do for His kingdom, and the more Satan will turn up the heat. But this increased pressure should help

you depend more and more on the Holy
Spirit as your source of strength.

◆ *Fallacy – You can always overcome temptation by running.*

One method of defending yourself against
potential temptations is by staying away from
likely sources of exposure. Yes, it is true that
avoidance of certain people and places helps
you gain the victory. The Bible tells us to flee
certain allures. (1 Timothy 6:11; 2 Timothy
2:22)

However, you cannot solve every problem
of temptation this way. People have left
churches, moved, or switched jobs just to get
away from situations that were threatening.
But they had the same difficulties in their new
environment as they did before. Why? They
never dealt with their desires honestly and
allowed the Lord to change them.

At times it is best to stay and face the conflict head-on, and sometimes it is best to turn
aside. Ask God for discernment about what to
do in your particular circumstances.

Recovery for Life

Jesus said: "Come to Me, all who are weary
and heavy-laden, and I will give you rest. Take
My yoke upon you, and learn from Me, for I
am gentle and humble in heart; and you shall
find rest for your souls. For My yoke is easy,

and My load is light." (Matthew 11:28-30)

Are you trying to make the right choices by yourself, or are you resting in Christ? Are you turning to His truth, or are you giving up without trying?

God's plan for you involves many seasons of moving through the steps of restoration outlined here. Do not be discouraged when you must start again. You will fail, and fail again, but Jesus is your new beginning.

Few things are sadder than seeing believers who refuse to learn from their mistakes. God wants to teach them how to walk in His ways, and they stubbornly try to move forward without His direction.

Do not waste your failures. Let the Lord turn personal trial into triumph, for yourself and for a living testimony to others of His victorious love and power.

Scripture Reference Guide for Handling Temptation

Anger

Ephesians 4:26-27   Proverbs 15:1
Proverbs 29:11   James 1:19-20
Romans 12:19

Appetite/Eating

Romans 12:1   Psalm 107:9

Philippians 4:13   Proverbs 23:20-21
1 Corinthians 6:18-20

Dishonesty/Stealing

Ephesians 4:28   Exodus 20:15
Proverbs 20:17   Psalm 86:11
Mark 7:21-23

Impatience

Galatians 5:22   Psalm 27:14
Psalm 40:1   Hebrews 10:35-36
Romans 8:25

Laziness/Lack of Motivation

2 Peter 1:5-7   Hebrews 6:11-12
Proverbs 6:6-11   Proverbs 10:4
2 Thessalonians 3:10-12

Lying

Colossians 3:8-10   Exodus 20:16
Ephesians 4:25   Proverbs 12:22
Psalm 119:142

Pride

Proverbs 16:18   Psalm 127:1-2
2 Corinthians 12:9   Ephesians 2:8-9
Jeremiah 9:23-24

Self-Esteem

Matthew 10:29-31   1 Samuel 16:7

Psalm 139   Philippians 2:3-5
2 Thessalonians 2:13

Sexual Desire
Matthew 5:27-30   Romans 13:13-14
Ephesians 5:3   1 Corinthians 6:18-20
1 Thessalonians 4:3-5

Speech/Language
Colossians 3:8-10   Luke 6:45
Ephesians 4:29   Proverbs 16:24
1 Peter 3:10

Thoughts/Thought Life
Philippians 4:8   Colossians 3:1-2
Psalm 119:11   Romans 12:2
2 Corinthians 10:4-5

Worry/Anxiety
Isaiah 41:10   1 John 5:14-15
Proverbs 3:26   Matthew 6:31-34
Philippians 4:6-8, 13

OVERCOMING
ADVERSITY

W hen the rain first started, it was just another inconvenience. Locate the misplaced umbrellas, drive a little more carefully, step gingerly around the puddles.

No one could have imagined the devastation that would follow. Unlike typical spring showers in the South, the rain didn't end very quickly. It continued to fall during the day and into night. It did not slack the next day either. For three days it fell steadily, saturating the ground, spilling into rising streams which fed gorged rivers that crested at record heights.

An entire town was flooded. Houses peeked above the muddy waters. Businesses were inundated. Lives, livelihoods, and lifestyles were dramatically altered. The reaction of residents was predictably emotional. What would they do? How would they recover? Could they?

Many months later, the media, which had reported the flooding almost nonstop at its peak, returned to report on how the townspeople had fared. Some were still in despair, unable to see much hope for the future. Others had survived, but there was an over riding atmosphere of pessimism in their voices. Yet remarkably, many had faced the disaster successfully. They were in the process of rebuilding and expressed confidence they would come out okay.

We can be grateful that few of us experience such large scale woe; but everyone, believer and nonbeliever alike, must deal with the problem of adversity. It can come in small, irritating packages that test our patience, as with a flat tire or a cranky coworker. Or it can arrive with fierce swiftness — the unexpected death of a spouse, a tragic car accident. Trouble to some degree does rain into everybody's life. Far more important than its magnitude or nature is our response to its blow.

Like the townspeople just described, we are emotionally and spiritually buffeted by distressing situations. But the Christian can actually advance through adversity, his trust in Christ strengthened by the painful process. Unlike the non-Christian, who may face and surmount dilemmas by sheer force of will and personality, the believer can deal with trauma from the perspective of faith in God's unchanging goodness and abundant help.

God always has a message for you in the storms. He will sustain you, guide you, and in His own way, use the adversity as His platform to display His love and power toward you in a very personal way.

Preparing for Adversity

Jesus made it clear: difficulties are to be expected. He told His followers in John 16:33: "These things I have spoken to you, that in Me you may have peace. In the world you have tribulation, but take courage; I have overcome the world."

Adversity is often the common thread that runs through the lives of the men and women mentioned in the Bible. Abraham, Moses, Joseph, Esther, David, Joshua, the prophets, the disciples, Elizabeth, Mary, Paul, and every other major biblical figure wrestled with problems. Adversity is a part of life. The consequences of sin are all around us. Although we can never be fully prepared for all the possibilities, we can take positive steps to fortify our faith to withstand the tough times.

The acceptance of setbacks is in reality a type of beginning. It is in acceptance that we truly recognize our need for God. Some things are much too tough for us to handle on our own. Paul could not preach the gospel to all of Asia Minor by himself. The Spirit of God was his constant companion through trials and tribulations, through laughter and reward.

Some evangelical Christians endorse a faulty viewpoint that goes like this: "If you will just trust God, and if your faith is right, and if you think right, then everything will be all right. God will simply deliver you."

In the end God will deliver each of us unto Himself in heaven, but this view does not adequately portray the Christian lifestyle, especially when adversity strikes. Often when trouble comes, it stays for a season of time. Paul struggled over the idea of having what he called a "thorn in the flesh" (2 Corinthians 12:7). We do not know what caused Paul's distress, only that God used it to draw the apostle closer to Himself.

Is there a thorn in your life? Something you have asked God to remove over and over again? Or did your thorn appear quickly and without much warning? Acknowledging that you struggle and hurt is not a blow to your faith or an admission of spiritual failure. On the contrary, it replaces pride with humility and positions you to exchange your weakness for Christ's strength (2 Corinthians 12:9).

The goal of suffering and adversity is to strengthen you spiritually by bringing you into closer fellowship with Christ. His word to you, especially if you are overwhelmed by your circumstances, is the same that He told those who followed Him: "Come to Me, all who are weary and heavy-laden, and I will give you rest. Take My yoke upon you, and learn from Me, for I am gentle and humble in heart; and you shall find rest for your souls.

For My yoke is easy, and My load is light"
(Matthew 11:28-30).

Another strategic step in preparing ourselves
to confront adversity is the exercise of daily
disciplines of faith. Jesus concludes His
Sermon on the Mount with this sobering
assessment. "Therefore everyone who hears
these words of Mine, and acts upon them, may
be compared to a wise man, who built his
house upon the rock. And the rain descended,
and the floods came, and the winds blew, and
burst against that house; and yet it did not fall,
for it had been founded upon the rock"
(Matthew 7:24-25).

The Christian is truly the best equipped to
deal with the harsh realities of life, for he has
attached himself to the right foundation — a
personal relationship with the Son of God. His
eternal destiny secured by the death of Christ
on the cross, he has access to all the resources
of God to handle the hard times.

That entails a solid regimen of reading and
studying God's Word, listening to His counsel,
and obeying His commands. It means prayer
and fellowship with other Christians should
have a high priority. We did not drift into salvation, and we will not drift into spiritual
maturity either. Deliberate decisions must be
made on a regular basis if we are to experience
the abundant life Christ promises. We may be
"afflicted in every way, but not crushed;

perplexed, but not despairing; persecuted, but not forsaken" (2 Corinthians 4:8-9). The J.B. Phillips translation says: "We may be knocked down, but we are never knocked out!"

In *Nevertheless, We Must Run Aground* Elisabeth Elliot wrote, "The story of Paul's voyage as prisoner across the Adriatic Sea tells how an angel stood beside him and told him not to be afraid (in spite of winds of hurricane force), for God would spare his life and the lives of all with him on board ship. Paul cheered his guards and fellow passengers with that word, but added, 'We must run aground on a certain island' (Acts 27:26).

"It would seem that the God who promises to spare all hands might have 'done the job right,' saved the ship as well, and spared them the ignominy of having to make it to land on the flotsam and jetsam that was left. The fact is He did not, nor does He always spare us.

"Heaven is not here, it's There. If we were given all we wanted here, our hearts would settle for this world rather than the next. God is forever luring up and away from this one, wooing us to Himself and His still invisible kingdom where we will certainly find what we do keenly long for. 'Running aground,' then, is not the end of the world." Accepting the reality of painful times while readying yourself to encounter them actually puts you at the starting block of great adventure in seeing

God's omnipotent hand work wondrously in your adversity.

Walking through the Darkness

Adversity's origins may vary. First, some hardships are the result our own actions. For example, we may be in financial straits because we have been poor stewards of the wealth God has provided. Other times, calamity is purely the scheming work of the devil. Job lost his family and health to Satan's malicious tactics.

However, just as it was in Job's life, all the adversity you face is sifted by the permissive, loving will of the Father. Ultimately, God allows suffering not for the purpose of defeating you, but to draw you to Himself for His purposes, which in the end are always good.

Rather than investing an inordinate amount of time deciphering the cause of your problem (unless, of course, you clearly need to repent of a willful sin), your concentration is better spent on a healthy response. You may never understand *why* something happens (Job didn't), but you can do something about *how* you respond. I can think of no better case study than the life of Joseph (Genesis 37–40). He is a classic example of God using adversity to promote spiritual growth and to accomplish His plans.

Sold into slavery by his jealous brothers, falsely accused by his Egyptian master of immorality and then dumped into prison,

Joseph spent thirteen years in what appears to us very unjust and degrading circumstances.

Joseph certainly could not fathom why all this was happening to him, especially since his dilemma was the result of the malevolent actions of others. Yet there is no scriptural indication that even hints that Joseph succumbed to bitterness and regret. We do not read about Joseph saying: "God, why have You done this to me? Why did You put me in this family? Why did You allow me to be sold as a slave?" Why did You allow me to be famed by Potiphar's wife?"

He may have pondered such queries in discouraging moments, but they did not occupy his energy or become his focus. Rather, Joseph sought to please God through his devotion and humble spirit. Therefore, God brought prosperity to Joseph's life and in the end made him second in command of all Egypt.

The Perspective of Providence

In the end, when his brothers came to beg for his forgiveness, Joseph viewed his ordeal in this transforming light: "And as for you [his brothers], you meant evil against me, but God meant it for good . . ." (Genesis 50:20). Joseph understood that God was ultimately in control of men and events, favorable as well as unfavorable ones. The arduous years of adversity were not wasted but instead were blended into God's providential plan for his life.

When life goes well, how often do you tell God that you truly need Him? God created us for Himself, but man rebelled and sought to find pleasure on his own. The distressful straits you may now find yourself in does not mean that God has abandoned you. He is with you and will see you through the pain.

The apostle Paul summed it up this way: "And we know that God causes all things to work together for good to those who love God, to those who are called according to His purpose" (Romans 8:28). This truth is hard to embrace when adversity hits. But it is the right orientation to restore hope when our troubles seek to douse it.

Theologian and author J.I. Packer depicts God's providence as "the unceasing activity of the Creator whereby, in overflowing bounty and goodwill, He upholds His creatures in ordered existence, guides and governs all events, circumstances, and free acts of angels and men, and directs everything to its appointed goal, for His own glory." What this means is that God's beneficent purpose for your life (which is to conform you to the image of Christ) will happen *progressively* as you trust Him.

Nothing comes to you by accident. Your adversity may be the result of another's mis-take, and you are struggling to accept the fallout. Yes, your burden is hard to bear, but if you truly know that God has allowed it and is actively working for your well-being right now, you can move forward.

"God gives only good," writes Margaret Clarkson in her book *Grace Grows Best in Winter.* "His will and His ways are perfect. If we believe these things implicitly, we must learn to make use of the strength they can impart. We must say them repeatedly to ourselves in our hours of darkness, laying them on our hearts as a healing balm, even though we may not feel their truth being borne out in our experience. . . . We set ourselves to believe in the overruling goodness, providence, and sovereignty of God and refuse to turn aside no matter what may come, no matter how we feel. God honors such faith. . . ."

I encourage you to affirm this truth now. "Lord, I believe that _____ is in your capable hands. I am grateful that You are in control and have not left me to fate, chance, or accident. Work through my pain and help me to see Your good. I realize this may take time, so sustain me in the days to come. Even if I never understand 'why,' I choose to trust You because You are always for me and never against me."

The Reason Not to Give Up

God's dictionary is certainly different. We think of adversity in fundamentally negative terms, but He does not. The apostle James wrote to Jewish believers scattered throughout Asia. They were under constant pressure for their beliefs, and no doubt they hoped James' letter would yield insights to alleviate their suffering.

James wasted little time in addressing their affliction, but probably it was not what his readers expected. "Consider it all joy, my brethren, when you encounter various trials, knowing that the testing of your faith produces endurance. And let endurance have its perfect result, that you may be perfect and complete, lacking in nothing" (James 1:2-4). What an odd twist on adversity. We are not to moan and groan when trouble slams against us, we are to "consider it all joy."

What is the first or second thing you think of when adversity strikes? Usually joy is not at the top of your response list. Scripture does not take a short-term view of adversity. It focuses on the long-term benefits of our pain, which, if we allow it, can be decidedly productive. The problematic situations you face now or have encountered in the past are not meaningless. They have purpose. Will you count on the surety of His promises when your spiritual knees wobble and shake?

The Christian life is one of extreme trust. We believe God has the ability to deliver and restore us even though the winds of adversity rake across our lives. Job, in the agony of his affliction, solemnly declared, "Though He slay me, I will hope in Him" (Job 13:15). This was the bottom line of Job's questioning.

There is an up side to adversity. Anchoring your trust in the Lord produces endurance and the ability to persevere. That is a tremendous asset in your spiritual walk. God is preparing you for a lifetime of devotion to Him, and each episode of adversity can contribute to your spiritual advancement (1 Corinthians 9:24-26). Enduring hardships strengthens you for the journey and leaves a legacy of solid faith.

Persevering through calamity is the way to spiritual maturity. It is the "perfect result" of endurance (James 1:4). The spiritually mature Christian has seen and dealt with his share of sorrow yet still possesses a radiant faith. He has been tested and tried and by God's grace has kept the faith. Thankfully, we have access to God's wisdom during our trials. This is why I believe James' encouragement to ask for God's wisdom immediately follows his exhortation to faith and perseverance.

Asking God for His insight is actually a way of expressing our dependence on Him (James 1:5). He may or may not choose to reveal the "why" behind our suffering; that is in His sovereign corner. But He is always willing to give us the daily wisdom we need to make good decisions and choices.

The fog of confusion is the densest in trouble. We easily can lose our spiritual bearings through poor decision-making. When we ask for God's wisdom, we are imploring God for His help, counsel, and guidance. He will keep us on the course of spiritual growth if we allow Him to lead us, teach us, and even rebuke us when necessary.

Time of Discovery

When conditions are consistently favorable, our spiritual learning curve is predictably flat. However, when thrust into turmoil, we quickly become eager students. Adversity serves as a great time to discover more about the character and nature of God. We learn He is good, faithful, merciful, sovereign, generous, and compassionate (Ephesians 2:4). His love is unconditional, not distributed on the basis of our performance (or lack of it).

This was Job's conclusion. "I know that Thou canst do all things, and that no purpose of Thine can be thwarted" (Job 42:2). This affirmation came in response to God's declaration of His power and sovereignty in the preceding chapters. Job realized the greatness of God and bowed to His sovereignty rather than linger in anger or cynicism. Let adversity drive you to God's bosom where you can find refuge and protection from the storm. Allow your struggles to propel you into deeper intimacy with the Savior. He will never disappoint you, condemn you, or fail you.

You also discover a great deal about yourself in affliction. The depths of the valley and the dark times reveal our true character. Is there an undetected hot spot of pride? Are you nursing some grudges against another, or even against God? Do you turn toward God or away from Him? Such self-examination, if not overdone, is profitable. Adversity strips away any veneers and exposes the "real you." It allows you to discern your value system and determine whether it aligns with God's purposes and principles.

Going Forward in God's Strength

Some can handle short doses of discomfort in their own strength. They can make it through a day or even a few weeks without feeling a substantial need for God's help. But when trouble comes to stay for a while, when it stalls out over your marriage, your work, your family and refuses to relinquish its grip, then your ability to cope may be severely diminished. It is then that you particularly desire and long for God's support.

In our weariness, we need to recall a vital truth — we can exchange our weakness for God's inexhaustible strength. Paul wrote of this amazing transfer. ". . . Most gladly, therefore, I will rather boast about my weaknesses, that the power of Christ may dwell in me. Therefore I am well content with weaknesses . . . for when I am weak, then I am strong" (2 Corinthians 12:9-10).

You can keep going when the going gets rough by receiving God's strength. This perseverance is the result of the indwelling life of Christ realized through the power of the Holy Spirit. In one of David's darkest moments, he wrote this beautiful psalm of praise to God:

"O God, Thou art my God; I shall seek Thee earnestly; my soul thirsts for Thee, my flesh yearns for Thee, in a dry and weary land where there is no water. Thus I have beheld Thee in the sanctuary, to see Thy power and Thy glory. Because Thy loving-kindness is better than life, my lips will praise Thee. So I will bless Thee as long as I live; I will lift up my hands in Thy name" (Psalm 63:1-4). Adversity brings us to the end of our self-sufficiency that we may experience the total adequacy of God for every demand.

I remember meeting the late missionary Bertha Smith at the airport when she was a spry seventy-two-year-old. I had gone to pick her up for a speaking engagement at our church, and I was amazed at how lively she was (she lived to be almost one hundred). At that time, she had the next five years of her life booked with meetings around the world. At the end of the first long day, Miss Smith was still going strong and I asked her, "Don't you ever get worn out?"

"I am not going in my strength," she replied. "I am going in God's strength." That was it. No fluffy theology, just straightforward honesty.

"Here's what I do," she said. "I just tell God what I have to do each day, and I let Him know I cannot accomplish it in my strength. On the surface, it may appear as if I can make it through the routine matter, but then I remember that Jesus said, 'You can do nothing apart from Me' (John 15:4-5). I then claim His power for each task, thank Him for it, and move on."

That may seem really simple, but it works. In your frailty, God is more than willing to uphold and sustain you. Your inner man will be fortified by power from on high. God will do it. You can count on Him. The prophet Isaiah wrote: "Yet those who wait for the Lord will gain new strength; they will mount up with wings like eagles, they will run and not get tired, they will walk and not become weary" (Isaiah 40:31).

The Wrong Response

Each of us can learn to respond to adversity correctly by asking God to teach us to see our lives and situations from His view and per-spective.

◆ *Refuse to blame others for your situation.* The problem may be instigated by another party, but you are only responsible for your reaction. The biblical pattern is always extending forgiveness, not assigning blame. You will miss God's blessing in adversity if you play the blame game. Remember that Joseph never retaliated against his brothers or Pharaoh despite their culpability.

◆ *Don't feel sorry for yourself.* This is an especially troublesome trap which accomplishes nothing positive. Self-pity is actually a subtle form of unbelief, for it certainly isn't conducive to confident faith. Encourage yourself through affirmation of God's faithfulness and love. Resist the temptation to slide down this slippery emotional slope by confessing the surety of God's Word and reminding yourself constantly of His great love for you.

◆ *Don't try to escape the problem.* You will not develop spiritual muscles by refusing to deal with problems. God is a wonderful problem-solver. He will not allow the weight of your burden to exceed your emotional, spiritual, or physical load limit. Many commit suicide as a way of escape, but this is not a viable option with God. If the notion enters your thinking, recognize its true nature — a lie from Satan. Suicide always causes great pain for friends and loved ones.

The Right Way

Adversity is emotionally or physically painful, but the pain can be for our benefit when we respond rightly. The following principles provide a framework that allow God to use your troubles for spiritual progress.

◆ *God never scolds you when you pray for release from your adversity.* It is only human to want relief. God understands this. Even Jesus in the Garden of Gethsemane prayed to be spared from the horror of separation from the Father. He is a sympathetic Savior who never has a condemning thought toward you. However, remember that your petitions for deliverance may or may not be answered the way you expect.

◆ *God will comfort you in your adversity.* Read the first chapter of 2 Corinthians. God knows how much encouragement you need and when you need it. He is the "God of all comfort." He will use Scripture, the kindness of others, a Christian radio or television program, a message from your pastor, or any other of His infinite ways to soothe your spirit.

◆ *You are never alone in your adversity.* God is ever present with you in the valley. "God is [your] refuge and strength, a very present help in trouble" (Psalm 46:1). A literal rendering of the latter part of that verse reads, "God is abundantly available for help in tight places." Jesus sustains you by being with you in your trouble.

◆ *Adversity is the best possible place to experience the grace of God.* God told Paul in his difficulty that "My grace is sufficient" (2 Corinthians 12:9). His Word is the same to you today. Someone has said that grace is "whatever you need, whenever you need it." Do you need wisdom? God's grace will provide it. Do you need inner peace? God gives it lavishly. God is your inexhaustible source of grace.

◆ *God's power reaches its peak at the lowest moments of our adversity.* When we exercise, the flow of blood is increased to the muscle groups used. The greater the demand, the greater the supply. The same law operates in the spiritual realm. The bigger our problem, the more of God's power flows to our aid.

◆ *God will use your experiences to encourage others in similar predicaments.* The person who has battled cancer knows exactly how another cancer patient feels. Words of comfort are laden with sympathy and meaning. You have "been there" and you do know the particulars of their struggle. Part of God's greater purpose in adversity is preparing you to help others who face similar problems. You become a man or woman who knows "how to sustain the weary one with a word" (Isaiah 50:4).

There Is Hope

The apostle Paul was a veteran of adversity. Life after his conversion to Christ was one calamity after another — beatings, shipwreck, stoning, imprisonment, to name a few of his adverse adventures.

Yet in the eighth chapter of Romans, Paul uttered this profound assertion of God's faithfulness in trials: "For I am convinced that neither death, nor life, nor angels, nor principalities, nor things present, nor things to come, nor powers, nor height, nor depth, nor any other created thing, shall be able to separate us from the love of God, which is in Christ Jesus our Lord" (Romans 8:38-39).

Whatever adversity you wrestle with today or tomorrow, you can be assured that you are never isolated from the love of God. Never give up in your adversity. Instead, give in to Christ and His love for you, and you will find yourself advancing through each and every hardship, moving from strength to strength.

"This I recall to my mind, therefore I have hope. The Lord's loving-kindnesses indeed never cease, for His compassions never fail. They are new every morning; great is Thy faithfulness" (Lamentations 3:21-23).

BEYOND
BITTERNESS

When you think of a stereotypically bitter person, most likely an image comes to mind of a surly, self-absorbed individual who can barely mutter a civil hello. The old-fashioned word "curmudgeon" is used to describe someone like this, with an almost ridiculously sour attitude and a cantankerous disposition.

A more modern phrase to describe this condition would be "having a chip on your shoulder." Some people walk around with a poor outlook, as though "somebody owes them something," and now they are taking it out on the world in general.

Bitter people like these are not difficult to spot; the results are obvious. What you would be surprised to learn, however, is that many, many people are "secretly" bitter. That is, they have a hidden attitude of bitterness that is a driving force in their mind, will, and emotions — and they don't know it.

What Is It?

Bitterness is a condition of the heart. In simple terms, it's deep-seated resentment that results from some past grief, disappointment, or emotional wound. Bitterness is a lack of forgiveness multiplied several times over, or an unforgiving spirit that takes root and spreads into every segment of life.

Have you ever seen a kudzu vine?

They grow well in the southern United States with the warm, humid weather. One little clipping — one tiny leaf with a root attached — digs into the soil and takes off. If it is not uprooted and killed immediately, it continues to grow at an astonishing rate. Wrapping its way around everything in its path, kudzu can easily engulf entire trees, smother their light source, and kill them. All of that destruction comes from one innocent-looking plant.

That is the way bitterness operates. It can grow out of a small and seemingly minor offense or a series of offenses. Once a spirit of unforgiveness sets in, all it needs is time and the fertilizer of a nursed grudge or an unresolved conflict.

A story is told of two sisters who did not speak to each other for more than twenty years. Why? You might think it was a serious issue that kept them apart, but the truth is quite the opposite. One sister had inadvertently done something inconsiderate to the other, who responded with some unkind words. Neither one asked forgiveness or attempted to reconcile afterward, and as the months passed, the emotions involved became so heated and intense that the offense was blown way out of proportion. We laugh at the notion of the "Hatfields and McCoys" feuding endlessly over nothing, but such is the fruit of bitter hearts.

Bitterness Is a Choice

A tragic side effect of bitterness is often a lack of perspective. Those who suffer from an unforgiving spirit begin to feel a false sense of powerlessness. They may believe that circumstances made them the way they are, and there is nothing they can do about it. Some even develop a complex of self-pity and seek the constant attention and sympathy of those who try to help them. When someone tells them to be thankful for what they have and move past the pain, they respond with a defensive statement such as: "But you don't know what I've been through," or "I deserve better than this."

It is crucial to understand that no one is obligated to respond to personal hurt or hard times with a resentful attitude. No one is forced to lash out in blame and reproach and cynicism when things go wrong.

If ever someone had an excellent excuse to be bitter, it was Fanny Crosby, the famous blind hymn writer who lived in the late 1800s. She was not born blind, however. Read in her own words the story of how her life was changed forever:

"When I was six weeks of age a slight cold caused an inflammation of the eyes, which appeared to demand the attention of the family physician; but he not being at home, a stranger was called. He recommended the use of hot poultices, which ultimately destroyed the sense of sight. When this sad misfortune became known throughout our neighborhood, the unfortunate man thought it best to leave; and we never heard of him again.

"But I have not for a moment, in more than eighty-five years, felt a spark of resentment against him because I have always believed from my youth to this very moment that the good Lord, in his infinite mercy, by this means consecrated me to the work that I am still permitted to do. When I remember his mercy and loving kindness; when I have been blessed above the common lot of mortals; and when happiness has touched the deep places of my soul — how can I repine?" (*Fanny J. Crosby: An Autobiography;* Baker Book House, 1986)

What an amazing response to an "unfair" tragedy. An event that would turn most people away from God actually moved this woman closer to Him. She even considered herself more blessed than other people. Such an attitude may seem incredible, almost superhuman, and in one sense, that's true. By ourselves, we can't look at difficulty and tragedy and hope to make sense of them. Part of the reason some people remain bitter about past pain is that they cannot find a reason for the pain in their own minds.

That is why a clear understanding of the principle of God's love is so crucial for working through issues of bitterness. When you belong to God — that is, when you have accepted Jesus Christ as your personal Savior — you have the assurance that suffering has a purpose. Romans 8:28 says: "And we know that God causes all things to work together for good to those who love God, to those who are called according to His purpose." This verse is a promise, a guarantee from the Lord Himself that He, in His wisdom and unfathomable love, is behind your circumstances and behind the event or words that caused you such pain.

A Profile of Pain

In the Old Testament, the once happy man Job becomes a case study in complete brokenness.

He is prosperous in every way. He has much money and property, a large and energetic, fun-loving family, and the respect and admiration of his entire community (Job 1). And unlike some who enjoy great material wealth, Job is not arrogant or pleasure-seeking; verse 1 says he is "blameless, upright, fearing God, and turning away from evil."

Then in rapid-fire succession, Job loses everything. All of his livestock are stolen or killed by ruthless nomads. His servants are slaughtered. His sons and daughters are crushed in a violent windstorm when the roof of the house caves in. Amazingly, Job does not fall apart in the sudden despair that assails him. His response of complete acceptance is famous: "Naked I came from my mother's womb, and naked I shall return there. The Lord gave and the Lord has taken away. Blessed be the name of the Lord." (1:21)

As if that were not enough tragedy for one man to handle, Job loses his health; his body becomes covered with boils from head to toe, accompanied by intense itching, fever, worm infestations, and aching bones (Job 1, 7, 30). His wife, practically the only person left who does not flee from him in disgust, asks him why he does not just curse the God who did this to him. Job answers her: "Shall we indeed accept good from God and not accept adversity?" (2:10)

Before you dismiss Job as an unrealistic example of blind obedience and humility, real-ize that the story of Job is far from over. All of these events take place by the second chapter, and there are forty-two chapters in the Book of Job. What happens next? Job spends much of the time answering three of his former friends when they tell him that he is being punished by God for some sin in his life. In defense of his innocence, and in the agonies of unrelenting physical pain and loss, Job falls into a common trap of those who suffer — he develops an attitude of bitterness.

"I will complain in the bitterness of my soul," he laments (7:11). In deep depression, he regrets the very days he was conceived and born, wishing that his mother had miscarried instead (3:11-13). As the false counselors continue to accuse him of secret evil, Job comes to believe that he is guilty of absolutely no wrongdoing before the Lord, which is untrue for all human beings.

Finally, a man who had stood in the background listening comes forward. His name is Elihu; because he is so much younger than Job and the others, he hesitates to speak (Job 32). Elihu's words are striking and just what the self-pitying Job needs to hear. Elihu is not uncompassionate; he recognizes the magnitude of Job's torture. But he also knows that Job has lost his perspective.

God in His sovereignty and love did not put suffering in Job's path without a point. He wants Job to cling to Him in utter dependence and submission, trusting in God alone to care for him and bring him out. Only when Job humbly acknowledges God's right to work as He chooses in his life can he begin to experience God's restoration (32:23-28).

At the end of the book, God Himself speaks to Job with power, directness, and

divine compassion. His words go straight to
the heart of Job's attitude problem. Job's
response is one of humble adoration: "I know
that You can do all things; no plan of Yours
can be thwarted. . . . My ears had heard of
You but now my eyes have seen You.
Therefore I despise myself and repent in dust
and ashes." (42:2, 5-6, NIV) God completes
the process of restoration by adding back to
Job perfect health and more wealth and family
than he had before. Any time we respond to
God's corrective guidance with a submissive
heart, He pours out His blessings on us.

Pain with a Purpose

The Book of Job is filled with rich insights
about the character of God and how He deals
with us, but the aim here is not to try to
explore the complexities of the problems
inherent in suffering. The vital point to
emphasize is the importance of recognizing
God's hand at work when you hurt. Before
you can move on to the steps of forgiving
those who were involved in inflicting the hurt,
you must deal with the ultimate issue of why
God sometimes works in your life through
events and words that wound your heart.

In her book *Help Lord, My Whole Life
Hurts,* Carole Mayhall addresses some common concerns about God's sovereignty in this
area:

"I've struggled and ached over the reasons people propose for pain. One heard frequently is, 'This is of Satan. God never intended it to happen.' An extension might be, 'If you had prayed harder, it needn't have happened.'

"To people who say that I want to yell, 'You mean it's my fault? You mean Satan has more power than God? You mean Romans 8:28 should read, "And we know that in all things God works for the good of those who love Him if you've prayed hard enough against the enemy"? But that negates the Word of God. How can you say that?' . . .

"In God's sovereignty, He sees the arrow of the enemy hurtling toward me. God could throw up a higher guard to ward it from me. But in His wisdom, He knows that this hard thing is necessary to form patience in my life. So God relaxes His guard and lets the arrow strike me just as He did with Job of old. . . .

"We will never be conformed to the image of Christ totally until we reach glory. But He is in the business of helping us shape up. There may be other reasons for the pain and suffering in our lives, but this is the ultimate one."

It's important to realize that nothing about your circumstances, whether past or present, is accidental. You don't wander in a maze of uncertainty, wondering if you will find the way through or if the outcome will be positive. God promises that He has only good in store for you (Jeremiah 29:11-13). Therefore, you can trust Him through the worst experiences imaginable and know that He takes care of you at every turn.

Take the Bitterness Test

As mentioned earlier, many people who suffer from an ingrained attitude of bitterness are not aware of their problem. Over time, it's easy for the heart and mind to attempt to justify long-held resentments as perfectly natural or harmless.

Bitterness always involves hatred in some form, of God or of some other person. You may be thinking, "I don't actually hate anyone." Hate is such a strong word; it can bring to mind pictures of someone committing murder in a fit of rage or resorting to some form of assault. But the real meaning of hate includes so much more than these overt actions. Ephesians 4:31 says: "Let all bitterness and wrath and anger and clamor and slander be put away from you, along with all malice." These attitudes and emotional conditions are all a part of hate and associated closely with bitterness.

You can test yourself to see if past hurt has developed into any deeper resentments. Questions such as the following may help you to begin to dig a little deeper into your heart.

♦ *Is there a painful memory that you cannot forget, no matter how hard you try to suppress the thought?*

♦ *Does this memory trigger the same emotional response today as at the time the original pain occurred?*

♦ *Do you replay the memory over and over, attempting to "live out" alternative responses and imagining what you might have said or done differently?*

♦ *Is there a person to whom you can't say kind words or extend common courtesy without feeling uncomfortable or irritated?*

♦ *Do you ever want to make someone "get what's coming" to him or her after a minor offense?*

♦ *Is there a physical place that you still avoid because something negative once happened to you there?*

If you answered yes to the majority of these, you may have a struggle with bitterness. When answering these questions, keep in mind that it is normal to remember past pain, and you are not unusual if you don't enjoy going back to a place that is associated with unpleasant events. You will never entirely forget what happened to you, but when the memory continues to be associated with intense, negative emotions, then you can be sure it has an unhealthy hold on your spirit.

Looking for the Cure

With every injury or mistreatment or heartache, you ultimately have two options: forgive the offender(s) completely or refuse to let go, believing that they owe you something to make up for what they did. In the short run, keeping them "on the hook" seems to be the easier and more gratifying choice, especially when the individual(s) are still involved in your life in some way.

You probably know by now that you cannot ignore past pain and simply hope that it will go away. The saying that "time heals old wounds" is a fallacy that has kept many from dealing with problems honestly and immediately. In fact, time actually causes old wounds to become infected and turn into a more serious emotional illness.

The poison of an unforgiving spirit damages the entire person. Someone with an angry heart is trapped in his own hostility, unable to give or receive love freely. Feelings are frozen, and this rigidity eventually affects others. The tension, anxiety, and guilt mounting on the inside are often expressed by sudden outbursts of frustration or criticism of family and friends. Often the blow-ups occur over a relatively small issue.

A woman who has had her feelings hurt by an unkind remark about her weight, for example, may not express her hurt to the person who made the remark. But the words rankle in her mind just the same. The next time she's out shopping and passes a slender woman, an ugly thought passes through her mind, leading her into further self-hatred. In this case, unresolved conflict turned to bitterness, which led to repressed anger and low self-esteem. The problem in the area of self worth will eventually affect all of the relationships in her life.

The only cure for a hurting heart is full and complete forgiveness. Nothing else does the job of genuine healing. The problem is that the very idea of forgiveness itself is threatening to us. After all, if you truly forgive someone, you let go of your right to hurt him in return; and the act of revenge seems as though it will bring great satisfaction, but the relief is short-lived.

If you feel that your pain runs too deep for you to forgive the offender out of the goodness of your heart — you're absolutely right. You aren't capable of forgiving in your own strength. Only Jesus can. Ephesians 4:32 says: "And be kind to one another, tender-hearted, forgiving each other, just as God in Christ also has forgiven you." You can forgive someone who has hurt you only on the basis of what

Jesus Christ did for you on the cross.

The One without sin died a cruel death in your place, taking all your sin on Himself to satisfy the eternal debt you owe to God (2 Corinthians 5:21). When you place your personal faith in Christ, recognizing what He did for you, and make Him your Lord and Savior, you are cleansed and released from all guilt (Romans 6:6-11). Your debt is paid in full, no matter how big your debt may be.

Through His grace, you can forgive others. You don't have the right to hold on to an offense or carry a grudge. When the Person with the greatest reason not to forgive paid the highest price in order to do just that, can you refuse to do the same? Your forgiveness of others is to be as free and unlimited as Christ's is for you.

In his book *Healing for Damaged Emotions,* David Seamands describes the link between the cross and the pain you carry.

"There is a scriptural way to deal with all these hurts from our past. God's way goes far beyond forgiving and surrendering resentment. God takes sins, failures, and hurts that happened earlier in your life and wraps His loving purposes around them to change them.

"The greatest illustration of this is the cross. There God took what, from a human standpoint, was the worst injustice and the deepest tragedy that ever happened and turned it into the most sublime gift man has ever known: the gift of salvation. . . .

"Are you part of debt-free community of Christians? . . . Every church should be a debt-free society, where we love each other because we are loved. Where we accept because we are accepted. Where we grace one another and are gracious because we have been graced, because we know the joy of having seen the Master tear up the charge card that we have spent beyond paying. . . .

"And so because He has set us free, we can set others free and thereby set in motion grace and love. The Apostle Paul summed it up in nine words: 'Owe no man anything, but to love one another' (Rom. 13:8)."

How Far Does Forgiveness Go?

Because forgiveness is essential to healing bitterness, we must learn to let go of the emotions we feel in this area. Extending forgiveness with no apparent boundaries may sound difficult, however, and even a little frightening. Doesn't forgiving someone regardless of his attitude leave you vulnerable? Can someone hurt you too many times or too deeply to be forgiven? The Apostle Peter struggled with these questions. He wanted to know how many times he had to forgive someone who offended him. Seven times was a generous offer, he thought. Just imagine Peter's surprise when Jesus said "seventy times seven" and told him an unforgettable story, recorded in Matthew 18:21-35.

A certain king decided to settle accounts with all his servants. Some owed him only a little money, but others owed him a great deal. One servant owed him ten thousand talents, which would be worth approximately $10 million today. Of course, this servant didn't have the money and could never repay that amount. In response, the king decided to sell the man and his whole family into slavery. When the servant begged for mercy, the king had compassion and canceled the debt completely.

What joy the fortunate servant should have felt! Instead, the first thing he did when he left the palace was to seize a man who owed him money and threaten him. This man owed the servant only a day's wages, yet the servant was unwilling to soften and sent him to debtor's prison. The servant obviously had no idea what unfathomable grace had been shown to him. He continued to cling to his book of accounts, even when his own slate had been wiped clean.

We can choose to live like the ungrateful servant, or we can choose freedom from the choke hold of bitterness.

What to Do About Bitterness

Once you've recognized that you are keeping resentments in your heart, and once you know that the only solution is forgiveness through the power of Jesus Christ, the last step is to obey and actually let Him do the work.

This process can be scary and sometimes awkward, especially if you have held on to a resentment for so long that it feels like a part of you. Many aren't quite sure how they'll feel once the intensity of the former emotion is gone. As you work through the issues surrounding forgiveness, be careful that you do not slip into believing some common fallacies about forgiveness.

Forgiveness is never justifying or excusing someone's wrongful actions towards you. Saying things such as, "She's had a rough life," "That's just the way he is," or "Well everyone makes mistakes," does not erase or minimize the offense. When confronted with the prospect of dealing straight-on with pain, some people even deny that the offense ever took place, or that somehow it was their fault and they deserved it anyway. But rationalization is ultimately a head-in-the-sand response that serves to compound the effects of bitterness.

So how should you confront someone who

has hurt you? Your approach depends to some degree on who the person is. Maybe it's a family member or close friend, someone you are near every day or see on a regular basis. Or perhaps the person lives too far away to be readily available. And it could be that the person has died, and you are denied the opportunity to ever talk face-to-face.

Every situation should be managed with this principle in mind: dealing with your bitter spirit should not bring harm to the offender. In certain instances, the abuse or hurt is so damaging that you would be wise to seek help from a pastor or professional Christian counselor. Whether you can arrange a talk in person or you must handle it within your heart, you need to set aside a special time to deal specifically with the pain.

As you look back at the offense, be honest about everything that you felt then and feel now. Don't hold back (except what would be inappropriate). State how you are hurting and the exact words or deeds that made you feel this way. As you do, you'll notice much of the anger begin to leave your system as the pent-up emotions are released.

Then you must consciously cancel the debt. Remember that this cancellation is an act of your will, not your emotions, which at this moment may be in a turmoil. Say aloud: "I choose to forgive you for . . ." and state the offense again. Conclude with a declaration such as, "I release you from this debt." When you meet the offender or confront the memory with an honest expression of emotion and dismiss all charges, you take the first step toward healing and renewal.

Beginning to Move On

Psalm 32:1 says, "How blessed is he whose transgression is forgiven, whose sin is covered!" The positive results of this time bring about a sense of freedom and exhilaration that are unmatched, especially if you have not known for a long time what it feels like to live without bitterness.

After you forgive the individual(s) who hurt you, you need to perform one more spiritual checkup to ensure that you have also forgiven yourself. Very often, hurts from the past involved your actions in some way, maybe a wrong reaction or an emotional lashing out. Even when you were in no way responsible for what happened, it is not uncommon to feel guilty or deserving of the misdeed.

When you forgive yourself or recognize the false guilt for what it is, you allow God to heal the personal brokenness. Feelings of shame may hide just beneath the surface of your emotions, erecting barriers that block your ability to receive God's love and the love of others. But God wants you to enjoy the freedom, security, and holiness that are yours right now in Jesus Christ. The hope-filled promise of Romans 8:1 belongs to you: "There is therefore now no condemnation for those who are in Christ Jesus."

Of course, you already know from experience that emotional pain is not just a thing of the past. As you live and grow in the Lord, you will certainly go through more times of hurt, sometimes as a result of deliberately harmful actions and words from those you trust. The principles of dealing with bitterness are always applicable; you can put them into action the moment an offense occurs. You don't have to "wait and see" if you have trouble dealing with the pain. Ephesians 4:26-27 says: "Be angry, and yet do not sin; do not let the sun go down on your anger, and do not give the devil an opportunity." A root of bitterness may spring up at any time if you are not sensitive to the Holy Spirit's leadership in relationships.

You will develop a lifestyle of love and the habit of forgiveness as you recognize your position in Christ, keeping His limitless mercy in mind. The Apostle Paul reminds us what our daily attitude should be. "It is a trustworthy statement, deserving full acceptance, that Christ Jesus came into the world to save sinners, among whom I am foremost of all. And yet for this reason I have found mercy, in order that in me as the foremost, Jesus Christ might demonstrate His perfect patience, as an example for those who would believe in Him for eternal life." (1 Timothy 1:15-16)

When you demonstrate the reality of what Christ did for you by forgiving those who hurt you, you enjoy the lasting blessing of a liberated heart. Most importantly, your bitterness-free spirit will point others to the ultimate Source of forgiveness and grace.

How to Handle Fear

One of my favorite stories illustrating fear is one told by a friend of mine. As a young boy he would cut through a vacant lot on his way home. One evening it was much later than normal when he began his trek. Halfway across the lot he heard someone following him. Each time he took a step his actions were mirrored perfectly in sound.

He tried fighting the feelings of fear that were welling up inside, but it was no use. His heart began beating faster. His stomach became tight, and his adrenaline began to flow. He tried walking faster, but whoever was following did so just as quickly. Finally, he stopped and turned to face his pursuer, but to his amazement no one was there. For a moment, he stood perfectly still and studied the terrain but saw nothing unusual. But as he turned to go he heard the noise once again. Suddenly, he realized what he was hearing was the rubbing together of his own corduroy pants!

Have you ever caught yourself in this position? Not necessarily running from corduroy, but being frightened by something that did not exist? Psychologists tell us the majority of the fears we feel never come true. They are thoughts or misbeliefs that come into our minds without basis, yet we choose to believe and many times go so far as to integrate them into our lives.

I have talked with people who struggled with a fear of failure. Many are successful businessmen and women, but for one reason or another they have a hard time shaking free of an overwhelming sense of doom when it comes to their future. In each instance, I asked God to help them reprogram their thinking from a position of negative misbeliefs to one of truth based on His Word. Fear is always subject to God's truth.

There may be times when it seems quite legitimate to feel fearful — a noise at night that awakens you and has you believing that someone is attempting to break in your home, or being stranded on an inner-city expressway late at night. However, from a Christian perspective, there is a time when fear has the right to overwhelm us. Christ never abandons us regardless of the situation. In fact, emergencies and sudden traumas are the very times when God wants us to sense His presence the strongest.

From time to time, I have well-meaning people suggest that I not address anything having to do with emotions but stick strictly to what is written in the Bible. I always chuckle a little inside because the same God that created you and me to love Him also equipped us with certain emotions.

Had He not given us emotions, then we would never be able to praise Him for who He is and for all His glorious attributes. Like any part of the Christian life, emotions must be kept in balance and be placed in subjection to Christ. If not, they will dominate our lives. Fear is one of those emotions, which just as in my friend's story, if left unchecked can motivate us to literally run from nothing more than a pair of corduroy pants.

Facing Our Fears

Each of us has felt fearful at some point in life. There came a time in my own life when I realized that I was struggling with fear. I was determined to find out the source. I knew if I did not, my ministry could suffer greatly because of it. As I prayed and asked God to reveal the cause of my fear, I found myself reliving memories from my childhood.

The early years of my life were turbulent. My dad died when I was two. My mother worked two jobs to ensure a roof over our heads and food on the table. The first memory I have as a child is one of fear, wondering if we would make it. I grew up cooking my own breakfast and packing my own school lunch. It was not my mother's goal to instill fear into my life. If anything, she taught me more

about faith than anyone else. It was the natural consequence of the circumstances surrounding me that bred instability and fear.
At night my mom and I would pray together. She taught me that even though times seem rough, God is in the midst of them ready to provide all we need. Mom trusted the Lord, and we never went hungry. There may have been lean times when our refrigerator was almost empty, but we had all that we needed.

None of us can afford to give the enemy a foothold in our lives. All Satan needs to harass us is an opportunity. Prayer and the Word of God are the most effective weapons we have against fear. When we acknowledge a sense of fearfulness to the Lord and ask for His protection and guidance, we position ourselves in faith.

Fear is a choice. It is amazing how many people tell me they are afraid they have committed the unpardonable sin. In spite of the fact that the blood of Jesus Christ cleanses them from all sin, there is still a haunting disbelief surrounding their lives. Usually, it all boils down to feeling guilty over some sin — either past or present. I then remind him or her of 1 John 1:9: "If we confess our sins, He is faithful and righteous to forgive us our sins and to cleanse us from all unrighteousness." God forgives us when we come to Him in humble prayer seeking His forgiveness.

More than likely, if a person insists on believing some fearful thought that is not true, his life will be riddled with fear. There is never a time when we have to worry whether or not God will forgive us. Every sin — all that we have ever done — is forgiven by His grace through the obedience of His Son at Calvary. Jesus died that we might have everlasting life. He has given us freedom, and there is no need to live in sin or fear.

In *The Sensation Of Being Somebody*, Maurice Wagner writes: "Fear paralyzes the mind, making us unable to think clearly. Fear of great magnitude disorganizes the mind temporarily so that confusion reigns. Fear also has a way of multiplying itself; we are so disabled when afraid that we become afraid of our fears. We cannot face problems when we are afraid of them. . . .

"It takes faith to master a fear problem. It is impossible to overcome fear by feeling guilty for the emotion. Nowhere in the Bible does God condemn a person for being afraid; instead He consistently encourages the fearful with such statements as, ['Do not fear; for I am with you'] (Isa. 41:10). When we are afraid, we feel all alone with our problem, and we feel overwhelmed. Faith accepts the fact that the problem is too much for us and also the fact that we are not alone in our problem; we have God with us."

In Luke 4:18, Jesus said: "The Spirit of the Lord is upon Me, because He anointed Me to present the gospel to the poor. He has sent Me to proclaim release to the captives." One of Christ's functions as Messiah is to bring release from oppression. Whatever is holding you captive must release its grip when you command it to do so in the name of Jesus Christ.

Sin or any emotional bondage cannot rule your life. The only power sin has in your life is the power you give it. It is a matter of choice. You can choose to sin and reject God's plan for your life, or you can choose to follow Christ in obedience. We are not destined to be sinful nor are we born to a life of fearfulness.

Doubt is a key contributor to fear. When we doubt God's ability to keep and provide for us, we become fearful. Many have adopted the view that man is the center of the universe. Everything that happens must be taken care of by man. However, the need to be in charge of our own destiny has a loophole in it. We are not all-powerful, nor can we keep certain events from taking place. Only God is sovereign. Ultimately, He is our only source of security.

Because we have trained ourselves to believe the lie that we are self-sufficient apart from God, fear runs rampant in our minds.

Instead of turning to God in prayer, our minds drift from one imagined problem to another. We try to fix everything and end up spiritually and emotionally exhausted.

Satan loves to get us running emotionally. He goes to great lengths to get us to imagine all kinds of things. Most of us can relate to losing a night's sleep to thoughts or worries that turn into fears.

A single thought can multiply and grow a thousand times over when it is watered by the enemy's lies. His chief objective is to cause you to stop trusting God. Once you do, he steals your sense of peace and hope. You begin to doubt the promises of God, and before you know it, fear has erected a power base in your life.

The Consequences Of Fear

In *Worry-Free Living*, Frank Minirth and Paul Meier of the Minirth and Meier clinic tell us one of the "most common words in the Greek language is the word phobos. [In Scripture fear is often interchanged with anxiety.] Many students of the Greek language draw correlation between this term phobos and phobe, the word for the mane of a horse, suggesting the idea of 'hair raising.' The field of medicine has long documented the physiological reaction of hair rising in response to fear, though the connection is not certain. Another concept involved in this word is to be startled and to run away, the idea of flight. . . .

"The essence of fear, thus, is a reaction to man's encounter with force, particularly a force more powerful than himself." Fear always is represented mentally by a show of strength much stronger than we are physically. When you worry about your son or daughter coming home safe from a date and they are late, fear cranks into action. Our brain tries to differentiate between what is real and what is fiction, but because we allow fear to creep in, our emotions rarely respond correctly.

The message we send our brains is one of alertness and danger. Our bodies respond physically with wet palms, a nervous stomach, a headache, paleness in skin color, and an overall posture of fear. Fifteen minutes later, when our son or daughter walks through the door, we pounce on him with the force of a stampeding herd.

You may be thinking, Well he or she should have been on time. But consider this — maybe we should trust the Lord a little more as well. There were times when my mother worried about our situation. The only way she could combat such feelings was to go to the Lord in prayer.

The consequences of fear are costly. The following is a list of some of the consequences we are almost certain to face if we remain in our fear.

Fear stifles our capacity to think and act properly.

Fear causes indecision.

Fear diminishes our capacity to achieve. People who are fearful often give up quickly.

Fear leads to panic — not rational acts.

Fear causes torment. We can become so engrossed by fear that we are blind to the change it has brought about in our lives. A person who is fearful worries about even the smallest of details, questioning if he or she has done the right thing. Remember Luke 4:18 — Jesus came to set the captives free.

Fear damages our relationships with others. If you have been deeply hurt by another person, you know the hesitancy involved in beginning another close relationship. But God doesn't not want us living in fear, especially when it comes to relationships. We were created for fellowship first and foremost with Him and then with others. No one is able to go through life without facing some hurt and disappointment.

Keeping our eyes on Christ, placing our trust in Him, and asking Him to provide solid beneficial relationships will help us open up to others. In some cases of very deep emotional hurt, there may be the need to forgive others and ourselves. Don't let fear keep you from experiencing God's best relationally. A pastor, Christian counselor, or trusted friend may be the help you need in reclaiming your ability to trust and eventually love others.

Fear damages our relationship with God. The only fear God wants us to have in our relationship with Him is a reverent fear of who He is. We are to worship Him and fear Him in His holiness. When we do this, we place ourselves in subjection to Jesus Christ. We acknowledge Him as our Lord and our need of Him in every area of life.

God does not want us to be afraid to come to Him about even the smallest of details. He is a personal, loving God who cares about everything that touches our lives. When we come into His presence, we enter the chamber of love and purity. Through His Son we have access to the holy of holies, where God abides eternally with those who love Him.

Fear interferes with our enjoyment of life. We cannot relax and look at life as pleasurable, because through the eyes of fear there is only darkness and impending doom. However, there is a cure for fear. You can be free, though it may take some time and willingness on your part. Fear cannot hold you captive any longer.

Is There a Way Out?

Yes! There is hope for the fearful. Reading back through the Scriptures reminds us that Jesus was very concerned for His disciples. They had been with Him for three years. All they had learned would be severely tested by His crucifixion. He was right. Moments after Christ's arrest, fear struck with a vengeance. The disciples went into hiding for fear of the same happening to them. Only John and Peter followed to see what would happen to the Lord.

Jesus was explicit with Peter. He told His impetuous disciple that his faith was about to be tested and that he would end up denying Him three times. Note that the opposite of faith is fear. Instead of arguing or rebuking Peter for what He knew would happen, Jesus offered a word that would one day be used to bring hope to Peter's heart — "I have prayed for you, that your faith may not fail; and you, when once you have turned again, strengthen your brothers." (Luke 22:32) But Peter missed the point and in verse 33 proclaimed: "Lord, with You I am ready to go both to prison and to death!"

Jesus took time to reassure His disciples that though He was about to leave them, He would return. In Peter's case, He even went so far as to give Peter a point of ministry when he had regained his faith footing — "strengthen your brothers."

Christian counselor Gary Collins writes: "Fears can come in response to a variety of situations. Different people are afraid of failure, the future, achieving success, rejection, intimacy, conflict, meaninglessness in life (sometimes called existential anxiety), sickness, death, loneliness, and a host of other real or imagined possibilities. Sometimes these feelings can build up in one's mind and create extreme anxiety — often in the absence of any real danger." One of his first suggestions in defusing fear and feelings of anxiety is a preventive one. "Coping with the causes of anxiety, when and before they arise, can prevent the development of [fear]."

Understanding the Cycle of Fear

How do we cope with fear? Is there a way out of the fear cycle? We begin by acknowledging we have a problem with fear, or that something has caused us to feel fearful. The next step is to identify the fear. Name it. If you are fearful because the future seems distant then write it down. Make a list of all your fears. Many of them may seem indefinable. This is normal and in keeping with the enemy's strategy against us.

Often he tries to oppress us with feelings and thoughts that are general and unattached to a single activity or event. This is why a person who struggles with feelings of depression will say, "Oh, I just feel down today," or "I feel depressed." There may not be a particular reason, just an overall impression.

Stop giving feelings such as these a place in your life. They belong to the enemy, and as a child of God you can place them in submission to Jesus Christ immediately. There is no scriptural basis for feeling fearful or depressed. God has given us His Word as a sure hope. Take each thought or feeling that you have written down and ask Him to provide a verse of Scripture that you can claim as a promise against the fear or feeling. It is God's will that you be set free from every fear.

A critical step in changing our fears into towers of faith is in learning to focus on the truth. If we are going to break the cycle of fear we must combat it with truth. The way we do this is to train ourselves to stop focusing on the negative and begin focusing on the positive.

I tell people that one of the most important things they can do in their spiritual walk with God is to keep a journal. This should be a place of honesty in which prayers, goals, and even fears are recorded on a regular basis.

If you list your fears, make sure that you list God's promises in Scripture to you as well. A good concordance or study Bible will help you do this. Admitting your fears to God and then seeking His wisdom concerning the issue are steps of faith. Faith always tugs at His heart strings; He loves to see His children reaching out to trust Him.

Another thing faith does is teach us to watch for God's leading. The way you train yourself to hear His voice is by learning to be still in your heart before Him. This involves meditating on Scripture. The Book of Psalms is a good place to begin. Select one that identifies in some way with your situation. Turn the psalm into a prayer or a praise to God. Changing the focus of your mind does not happen overnight. Breaking through the fear barrier takes time, but along the way God promises to be with you, encouraging you and protecting you as you go. (Joshua 1:8-9; Psalm 23:4)

The final step in changing your fears into faith is to ask God to help you trust Him to a greater degree. Personal relationships can require a great deal of faith. One woman came to me years ago struggling with an overall sense of fear. All she could talk about was what she was feeling. As we worked through those feelings, we discovered that she had a spirit of unforgiveness against another person. Her lack of forgiveness in one area branched into other areas of her life. She truly wanted to be free, but resentment and bitterness had her bound.

How did a lack of forgiveness lead to her fear? As she refused to forgive the person who had hurt her, she became insistent on telling her side of the issue. The more she told the story, the more she dwelled on the subject mentally. What she was really doing was questioning her actions. Deep inside, her self-esteem was being eroded, which led to feelings of uncertainty. Before she knew it, she was lying awake at night trying to reassure herself, but all the while fighting feelings of anxiety.

None of us has to be a victim of fear. Faith in Christ is our strong tower. I have three principles given to me by my grandfather, ones I have adopted into my life and live by each day.

• Obey God and leave the consequences of life to Him. He has been in control of everything since the beginning of time, and He is not about to abandon His plan for you now. (Psalm 138:8)

• God will move heaven and earth to reveal Himself and His will to you. However, you have to want to know what He says. His responsibility is to make Himself available; yours is to respond to His availability.

• God provides for all your needs. God promises in Philippians 4:19 that He will provide for all your needs. You have the wondrous privilege of coming to Him with every need in full confidence that He will provide for you perfectly.

A college student once shared with me how he had trusted God to meet his financial needs for the upcoming semester. He wasn't sure if he would receive the grants he needed to cover his tuition costs. As the day for registration approached, he began to worry about what would happen should the money not be there. Soon these thoughts gave way to fear. Finally, he prayed: "Lord, You brought me here, and I'm going to start trusting You right now. I know You have all the money that I could possibly need for college. Please meet that need in Your way and in Your timing."

The next day he went to register for classes without a dime in his pocket. Standing in line, he continue to pray silently and refused to listen to the prodding of the enemy that he was about to be asked to leave school. As he approached the financial aid table a counselor looked up at him and smiled: "John, you received your grants for tuition, and the college has given you a two hundred dollar grant as well." He could hardly contain himself. The amount was just what he needed. The unexpected college money would be used to purchase his books for class.

When you place your trust in God, you will never be disappointed. God always provides for your needs.

People who fight feelings of fear overlook the fact that God is sovereign, omniscient, omnipresent, and infinite in power. He never changes — He is the same yesterday, today, and tomorrow. Whatever happens, God is never out of control. It is true; He holds the whole world in His hands. Psalm 100:3 says: "We are His people and the sheep of His pasture." Psalm 23 says: "Even though I walk through the valley of the shadow of death, I fear no evil; for Thou art with me; Thy rod and Thy staff, they comfort me. Thou dost prepare a table before me in the presence of my enemies; Thou hast anointed my head with oil; my cup overflows. Surely goodness and loving-kindness will follow me all the days of my life."

In a hymn Charles Wesley wrote —

> *Arise, my soul, arise;*
>
> *Shake off they guilty fears;*
>
> *The bleeding Sacrifice*
>
> *In my behalf appears:*
>
> *Before the throne my Surety stands,*
>
> *My name is written on His hands.*

> *My God is reconciled;*
>
> *His pardoning voice I hear;*

He owns me for His child;

I can no longer fear:

With confidence I now draw nigh,

And "Father, Abba, Father," cry.

No matter what happens in this world, you can trust God to guide you and give wisdom to make the right decisions. There is no need to lie awake at night and fret about tomorrow, because tomorrow is already taken care of by your Lord and Savior.

If you think you are struggling with fear or anxiety, go to Him in prayer right now. Tell Him that you love Him and are willing to let go of your personal claim to your life. Picture yourself handing the reins of your life over to Him. Ask His forgiveness for the times you acted in fear and panic without coming to Him in trust.

Then spend a few moments looking up the following Scriptures that reaffirm His love and care for you. Remember, God loves you with a perfect love, and "perfect love casts out fear" (1 John 4:28).

Deuteronomy 31:8

Isaiah 8:12

Psalm 27:1-3

2 Timothy 1:7

John 14:27

Isaiah 41:10, 13